Cambridge Elements

Elements in Business Strategy
edited by
J.-C. Spende
Kozminski Univer

DYNAMIC CAPABILITIES AND RELATED PARADIGMS

David J. Teece
University of California, Berkeley

Shaftesbury Road, Cambridge CB2 8EA, United Kingdom

One Liberty Plaza, 20th Floor, New York, NY 10006, USA

477 Williamstown Road, Port Melbourne, VIC 3207, Australia

314–321, 3rd Floor, Plot 3, Splendor Forum, Jasola District Centre, New Delhi – 110025, India

103 Penang Road, #05–06/07, Visioncrest Commercial, Singapore 238467

Cambridge University Press is part of Cambridge University Press & Assessment, a department of the University of Cambridge.

We share the University's mission to contribute to society through the pursuit of education, learning and research at the highest international levels of excellence.

www.cambridge.org
Information on this title: www.cambridge.org/9781009618410

DOI: 10.1017/9781009232890

© David J. Teece 2025

This publication is in copyright. Subject to statutory exception and to the provisions of relevant collective licensing agreements, with the exception of the Creative Commons version the link for which is provided below, no reproduction of any part may take place without the written permission of Cambridge University Press & Assessment.

An online version of this work is published at doi.org/10.1017/9781009232890 under a Creative Commons Open Access license CC-BY-NC 4.0 which permits re-use, distribution and reproduction in any medium for non-commercial purposes providing appropriate credit to the original work is given and any changes made are indicated. To view a copy of this license visit https://creativecommons.org/licenses/by-nc/4.0

When citing this work, please include a reference to the DOI 10.1017/9781009232890

First published 2025

A catalogue record for this publication is available from the British Library

ISBN 978-1-009-61841-0 Hardback
ISBN 978-1-009-23288-3 Paperback
ISSN 2515-0693 (online)
ISSN 2515-0685 (print)

Cambridge University Press & Assessment has no responsibility for the persistence or accuracy of URLs for external or third-party internet websites referred to in this publication and does not guarantee that any content on such websites is, or will remain, accurate or appropriate.

For EU product safety concerns, contact us at Calle de José Abascal, 56, 1°, 28003 Madrid, Spain, or email eugpsr@cambridge.org

Dynamic Capabilities and Related Paradigms

Elements in Business Strategy

DOI: 10.1017/9781009232890
First published online: June 2025

David J. Teece
University of California, Berkeley
Author for correspondence: David J. Teece, dteece@thinkbrg.com

Abstract: Of the numerous theories of strategic management, the dynamic capabilities framework is perhaps the most encompassing. Dynamic capabilities are the factors that, if strong, allow an organization to create and deliver value to customers, outcompete rivals, and reap financial rewards over extended periods. The dynamic capabilities framework provides a system-level view of how resources and capabilities are assembled and orchestrated over successive rounds of competition, addressing management's role in determining future requirements and honing the organization's processes and structure to meet them.

This Element presents the dynamic capabilities framework and compares it to other paradigms of strategic management and innovation. It demonstrates that these narrower approaches to strategic management and innovation can usefully be thought of as subsets of the dynamic capabilities framework. This will help students and practitioners understand disparate business concepts as part of a unified whole. This title is also available as Open Access on Cambridge Core.

This Element also has a video abstract:
www.cambridge.org/EBUS_Teece_abstract

Keywords: competitive advantage, dynamic capabilities, entrepreneurial management, innovation, strategy

© David J. Teece 2025

ISBNs: 9781009618410 (HB), 9781009232883 (PB), 9781009232890 (OC)
ISSNs: 2515-0693 (online), 2515-0685 (print)

Contents

1 Introduction   1

2 Capabilities: An Introduction   7

3 Dynamic Capabilities   23

4 Related Paradigms   40

5 Conclusions   63

    References   68

1 Introduction

Business schools around the globe teach a wide variety of disciplines, subdisciplines, methods, and models. Many of the disciplines, such as finance, human resources, and marketing, outline and explain how to manage the everyday activities that every company must perform competently. But, by themselves, the techniques and tools proffered, even if practiced at a high level of proficiency, seldom allow a company facing competition to pull ahead.[1] Moreover, they are generally taught, or implemented, by specialists in each area who may not employ an overarching framework that allows easy integration of their ideas into the bigger picture of corporate success or failure.

This Element arose because of an invitation from the Business Strategy series editor to write an Element covering a big-picture approach to management called the dynamic capabilities framework. In the end, two Elements were needed, this one, which includes an introduction to the framework and a comparison to other approaches to strategic management, and a companion Element presenting a capabilities-based "theory of the firm" and the relationship of dynamic capabilities to older, foundational concepts in the business and economics literature.

The goal of the two Elements is to help scholars and practitioners of management gain a deeper understanding of dynamic capabilities – currently the dominant paradigm in strategic management – and their relation to other concepts and models of the firm. The books' intended audience includes teachers of strategic management and managers ("practitioners") who may have encountered some of these concepts in classrooms, journals, or in the real world.

Strategic management is a relatively new subdiscipline that focuses on the high-level, interconnected clusters of decisions that determine the longer-run success or failure of business enterprises. But, even in this field, a plethora of concepts and models are taught by a range of practitioners, economists, and other specialists who may not have the desire or even the ability to connect the disparate elements in a coherent and practical manner.

The dynamic capabilities framework is a high-level systems theory approach to the strategic management of the enterprise that tries to address these deficiencies.[2] It emerged in the 1990s and has continued to evolve and to

---

[1] The disciplinary, recipe-based approach to management treats competition almost like a game of chess. Competition in the global economy is more reminiscent of (early) mixed martial arts, where multiple combat disciplines, like karate and kickboxing, are allowed. In its early iterations, there were few rules, and fighters could use any combination of fighting styles.

[2] Systems theory views organizations as social systems whose elements must be coherent if the organization is to be effective (Churchman, 1968).

drive research. In the view of some strategic management scholars, "the dynamic capabilities perspective has firmly established itself as one of the most influential theoretical lenses in contemporary management scholarship" (Schilke, Hu, and Helfat, 2018, p. 390).

The dynamic capabilities framework encompasses capabilities (what the company can do), resources (the assets the company controls), and strategy (how the company selects products and markets, delights customers, and pleases partners). In addition, the framework explicitly incorporates, complements, or augments other concepts, models, and paradigms from the field of strategic management and beyond.

Dynamic capabilities reside in the minds of managers and, to a lesser degree, in the routines and traditions of the organization. Adroit orchestration by top management of the organization's capabilities and resources over time is essential for increasing the odds that an organization will maintain a profitable competitive advantage over time, even as it shifts its activities across product and service lines and rides out waves of economic and technological change. Dynamic capabilities can be exercised at the level of a business unit as well as for a whole company – or even for a government (Mazzucato and Kattel, 2020).

In practice, competitive advantage is often fleeting. A firm's management sometimes develops and orchestrates a compelling combination of tangible and intangible assets that sees it on top for a few years before its products and services lose their currency with customers or rivals erode its position. But a few large, long-lived firms make astute, bold bets to open new markets and develop internal systems to help them manage shifts in consumer taste, revolutions in technology, and successions in leadership. Companies like ICI, 3M, IBM, Boeing, GE, NEC, and Nokia had long, profitable runs that made clear they were not one-hit wonders. Yet even they have each now lost much of their luster. Some of this is down to luck, which is an element in any business outcome. While luck sometimes turns very bad, it also tends to favor the prepared.

Many other, lesser-known companies have also built lengthy records of success. Paint and coatings maker Sherwin-Williams, recently added as one of the thirty companies in the Dow Jones Industrial Average, is still going strong after more than 150 years of innovation and growth, with occasional crises that it has surmounted. Records like these don't prove that a particular company has strong dynamic capabilities. Yet, it is hard to imagine a history of any long-lived enterprise that couldn't be usefully understood in dynamic capabilities terms. Dynamic capabilities are, at root, about maintaining a company's fit with its environment over time, which requires the ability to change. Any company that has performed well on average over a very long period has done this by definition. Any single success can be luck or a flash of entrepreneurial insight, but a record of decades of success under a string of leaders suggests that there's something in the organization's culture and processes that helps it select the right leadership, makes it more adaptable than its rivals to shifts in the business environment, and allows it to shape that environment, forcing rivals to adapt.

Dynamic capabilities are presented here as part of a broader framework. This framework is not a model, nor is it a theory. It is more general than either of those. In her Nobel Prize address, economist Elinor Ostrom positioned frameworks as part of a nested hierarchy. A framework constitutes the broadest level and contains "the most general set of variables that an institutional analyst may want to use to examine a diversity of institutional settings including human interactions within markets, private firms, families, community organizations, legislatures, and government agencies." Within a framework, "[a] theory is used by an analyst to specify which working parts of a framework are considered useful to explain diverse outcomes and how they relate to one another" (Ostrom, 2010, p. 414). Within the ambit of a theory, "models make precise assumptions about a limited number of variables in a theory that scholars use to examine the formal consequences of these specific assumptions about the motivation of actors and the structure of the situation they face" (ibid.).

As a framework (i.e., a broad array of variables that can be used to spawn useful theories), the dynamic capabilities framework is extremely ambitious, seeking to explain the roots of the competitive advantage (or its absence) of particular firms. This is a most fundamental business and economic question. By design, the dynamic capabilities framework is sufficiently general that many other approaches to the securing of competitive advantage can be seen as using subsets of the variables within it, potentially unifying somewhat fragmented fields of knowledge.

Adam Smith's *Wealth of Nations* (1776) was developed from studying the interplay of business operations, workers, and nation-states at the dawn of the Industrial Revolution, informed by Smith's knowledge of history back to Greek and Roman civilizations. In a similar manner, the dynamic capabilities framework was formulated by observing the development of Silicon Valley's leading enterprises as they delivered extraordinary growth and profitability. At the same time, many earlier corporate histories provided positive – and negative – examples because much that is old can become new again. The analysis of this observational data was informed by existing developments in organization theory, behavioral economics, business history, and (strategic) management.

There is no question that technological shifts, particularly digitalization, have impacted competition and strategy and will continue to do so. But the fundamental organizational, technological, and competitive forces captured in the dynamic capabilities framework still apply. In fact, the system-level thinking of dynamic capabilities is even more important in a digital setting. Digitalization facilitates global transactions, but it creates new vulnerabilities, such as cybercrimes. In July 2024, a small corner of the digital supply chain imploded when a CrowdStrike software update failed, negatively impacting airlines, border crossings, and health services across multiple jurisdictions. Agile and effective sensing and interpretation of signals is more urgent than ever in an interconnected and interdependent global economy.

The central thesis behind the dynamic capabilities framework is that, in a global economy facing deep uncertainty, active asset orchestration (i.e., continually assessing, modifying, and coordinating internal and external resources) by entrepreneurial managers, coupled with good strategy and a bit of good luck, can enable the business enterprise to generate and capture supernormal profits over the long term. Success is not just about achieving economies of scale and scope or generating network effects. These factors are, of course, important. But outperforming rivals over the long term comes from keeping the firm's asset base aligned with its strategy and shaping the evolution of the business environment and the firm's ecosystems.

To achieve this, entrepreneurial managers must exercise good judgment and make decisions with less than full information. While managers may have rules of thumb for strategy that are rooted in the company's culture and history, strategic decisions typically flow from creative improvisation rather than from a decision-making routine (Bingham and Eisenhardt, 2011). Many strategic decisions cannot be routinized because they occur infrequently, and most are unique. This has been the case since the rise of the modern corporation in the Second Industrial Revolution that began in the late nineteenth century.[3]

Entrepreneurial managers and routine-based managers are complementary. The first category supports dynamic capabilities, while the second supports ordinary and superordinary capabilities. Both are necessary if large, multidivisional, and/or vertically integrated enterprises in competitive markets are to master routine efficiency, while its leadership addresses ever-increasing levels of productive and competitive complexity.

General Stanley McChrystal, who oversaw US forces in Iraq and Afghanistan from 2003 to 2008, recognized the need for combining team-level efficiency with overall asset orchestration in the service of a strategy: "We had a culture in

---

[3] There is a debate in the academic literature about the rise of the corporation. The dominant view (associated with Alfred Chandler and Oliver Williamson) holds that corporations exploiting new technologies expanded vertically to minimize transaction costs. A more recent interpretation of the relevant history is that the expansion was driven by entrepreneurial experimentation with access to limited information (Casson and Godley, 2007).

our forces, of excellence ... How good can I be at flying an airplane, dropping bombs, locating an enemy target? But that's not as important as how well those pieces mesh together" (Rose, 2013). And he saw the need for this orchestration to extend beyond the boundaries of the organization: "The real art is [in] cooperating with civilian agencies, it's cooperating with conventional forces, it's tying the pieces together. That's the art of war, and that's the hard part" (ibid.).

The popularity of the dynamic capabilities framework is undoubtedly due to how well it resonates with today's business environment, which is characterized by rapid technological change, uncertainty in the regulatory domain, and now also in the geopolitical sphere as the world economy – previously knit together by nearly frictionless globalization – unravels. The framework endeavors to embrace the observed complexity without entirely sacrificing parsimony.

The founding definition of dynamic capabilities was "The ability of an organization and its management to integrate, build, and reconfigure internal and external competences to address rapidly changing environments" (Teece, Pisano, and Shuen, 1997, p. 516). The emphasis in 1997 was on technological innovation as the generator of change, but dynamic capabilities are equally vital for addressing deep geopolitical uncertainty and changes in governance and regulatory environments at home and abroad (Teece, Peteraf, and Leih, 2016; Teece, Gupta, and Rosenberg, 2023).

Complexity, competitive opaqueness, and ubiquitous interdependencies in the global economy are why building and practicing dynamic capabilities is hard but necessary.[4] Even articulating it is a challenge. In this regard, it conforms to a sentiment expressed by Albert Einstein that is often paraphrased as "everything should be as simple as it can be but not simpler."[5] The dynamic capabilities framework draws ideas from multiple literatures, not just in management but also in economics and psychology. It cannot easily be reduced to memorable slogans, but, where possible, I'll try to provide them.

A key goal of this book is to show how disparate approaches to strategic management, which are frequently taught to business students in isolation, can be seen as part of a unified whole: the dynamic capabilities framework. Although not addressed here, dynamic capabilities thinking can equally be

---

[4] Companies must develop sensitivity in order to detect "unseen" opportunities and threats. The title of former Intel CEO Andy Grove's book, *Only the Paranoid Survive* (Grove, 1996), captures the level of alertness required.

[5] See https://quoteinvestigator.com/2011/05/13/einstein-simple/. The original quote, from a 1933 lecture, is "It can scarcely be denied that the supreme goal of all theory is to make the irreducible basic elements as simple and as few as possible without having to surrender the adequate representation of a single datum of experience."

applied to human resources, marketing, and other business functions, each of which must be aligned with the strategy of the enterprise if it is to be effective.

Many of the principles underlying the dynamic capabilities framework have been common currency in the business world over the years. For example, a book called *Who Moved My Cheese* (Johnson, 1998) became popular in the late 1990s and provided a parable about the need to innovate and change in order to achieve a desired goal. A team named Hem and Haw go hungry compared with a team named Sniff and Scurry, who are not overly attached to past success, respond to circumstances as they evolve, and embrace change as part of life. In capabilities terms, Hem and Haw are attached to their (quite ordinary) capabilities, while Sniff and Scurry engage in the sensing, seizing, and transforming that are, as will be explained, the essence of dynamic capabilities.

There is a penchant in the academic world – and sometimes in business as well – to advance silver bullet solutions to complex problems, and to do so without analyzing their relationship to existing ideas and concepts. Management ideas are too often left unconnected by their authors or by the professoriate to broader concepts or related ideas. This is unhelpful to the reader and misleading to the decision maker. This Element aims to help scholars and practitioners alike struggle through the cacophony. Among the goals in the pages that follow are to uncover hidden assumptions, identify boundary conditions, and show the consistency of common Silicon Valley management ideas with the dynamic capabilities framework.

The remainder of this Element begins with a recap of the dynamic capabilities framework. There have been countless additions by other authors to dynamic capabilities scholarship. I have also written dozens of articles and given many talks on various aspects of the topic (uncertainty, business models, etc.) as the framework has continued to evolve, deepen, and strengthen. This Element represents the most up-to-date version of the framework in a compact form. Relevant articles are referenced throughout for those interested in delving deeper.

After that, I briefly sketch a dozen strategic management paradigms related to innovation, strategic positioning, and organizational design and compare each of them to the dynamic capabilities framework, drawing out similarities and differences. In three instances, two paradigms are discussed together to underscore key similarities.

The penchant of strategic management authors, including me, for touting their own solutions in isolation from even the more prominent among the many competing and complementary ideas has sown confusion among scholars and practitioners. This Element is an effort to help remedy the situation, for myself as well as for others.

2 Capabilities: An Introduction

A capability is the potential to bring about an outcome. Firms have assets, but money, employees, and patents do not by themselves produce goods and services. Rather, production requires assets to be orchestrated by managers into organizational capabilities that can then be harnessed toward strategic goals. Well-orchestrated capabilities allow firms to delight customers, yield revenue, and generate profits. The managers of government agencies and nonprofit organizations such as universities must exercise their (dynamic) capabilities, too, if they are to achieve their strategic goals and maintain long-run evolutionary fitness (Leih and Teece, 2016).

Capabilities are key to the performance not only of firms but also, ultimately, of nations. John Sutton of the London School of Economics states in his book *Competing in Capabilities* that "The proximate cause [of differences in the wealth of nations] lies, for the most part, in the capabilities of firms" (Sutton, 2012, p. 8). As work like this shows, an embrace of capability thinking, a seemingly simple, yet powerful and transformative, concept, is steadily spreading beyond the field of strategic management, where it already has very strong currency. Sutton's statement, for example, has profound implications not only for economic theory but for economic development policy, which has sometimes emphasized the accumulation of capital stock over the development of business enterprises with strong organizational and technological capabilities.

One scholar defined an organizational capability as "*a high-level routine (or collection of routines) that, together with its implementing input flows, confers upon an organization's management a set of decision options for producing significant outputs of a particular type*" (Winter, 2000, p. 983, italics in the original). This conveys a key point; a capability is something valuable that the organization, and/or its current top management team, has learned to do that is subject to management control. In other words, an organizational capability is a type of intangible asset (Teece, 2015). However, as will be discussed later, unique management decisions – often arrived at by reasoning from first principles – are also part of a firm's capabilities. Management is constrained in the short term by what the organization knows how to do, but management can also decide to change, over time, what the organization can do.

Capabilities are also resources in the "resource-based view" sense described by others (e.g., Wernerfelt, 1984). A key for connecting dynamic capabilities to competitive advantage is explaining why some capabilities are value-enhancing and difficult for rivals to imitate. Before addressing that, though, it's worth looking again at why the dynamic capabilities framework was created and how it has evolved.

2.1 Why We Needed a New Framework

The dynamic capabilities framework was created because existing approaches to explaining how firms built competitive advantage fell short of reality. This is particularly true in the case of entrepreneurial, Silicon Valley-style firms. These firms depend more than most on outsourcing, platforms, and alliance/ecosystem partners, indicating a need to understand management of external as well as internal resources. Furthermore, they often represent the cutting edge of strategic management and are able to advance rapidly in environments of deep uncertainty, animated, in the first instance, by rapid technological change.

Uncertainty is worth underscoring because it's different from risk. Risk can be calibrated, managed with standard risk management tools, and, in many cases, insured against, since actuarial values can be calculated using estimated probabilities. Uncertainty, by contrast, represents the unpredictable, meaning occurrences that are currently unforeseeable with impacts that are unquantifiable. When such events occur, strong dynamic capabilities enable organizations to respond by shaping the altered competitive environment rather than being shaped by it.

The dominant models of strategy in the 1990s, Michael Porter's Five Forces (discussed in Section 4.2.2) and the Resource-Based View (discussed in the companion Element on *Foundational Concepts*), were too static and tended to ignore uncertainty. Once a firm had achieved an advantage through clever positioning or by acquiring the right assets, it could switch to autopilot. But these theories were missing the reality that firms increasingly had to keep moving faster and smarter just to stay competitive, a phenomenon known as the Red Queen effect (Barnett, 2008). The Porter framework gave short shrift to heterogeneity within each industry and also ignored the strategic implications of complementary assets (discussed in *Foundational Concepts*), which are critical in the digital economy.

The first major dynamic capabilities articles[6] (Teece and Pisano, 1994; Teece, Pisano, and Shuen, 1997) emphasized the evolutionary aspects of capabilities, placing knowledge and learning at the heart of capability development. In so doing, they also highlighted the difficulty of making strategic changes when needed, because new capabilities take time to nurture and build (or to access, if external).

The recognition of the importance of learning to dynamic capabilities represented a shift from the resource-based view, which emphasizes the accumulation of valuable resources. The resource-based view (discussed further in the companion Element on *Foundational Concepts*) also downplays the need for

---

[6] The lineage of these articles can be traced back to a working paper (Teece, Pisano, and Shuen, 1990).

asset orchestration both inside and outside the organization, another key plank in the dynamic capabilities framework. This includes the nurturing of business ecosystem relationships to drive (mutual) learning and success.

In practice, the firm's history of investments and learning can make its path to the future either easier or harder, depending on the degree of match at a given time between the firm's capabilities and the requirements of the business environment. When the release of OpenAI's ChatGPT in October 2022 ignited massive interest in generative artificial intelligence, Nvidia not only had the best chips and associated software for powering such systems, it had a well-established outsourcing relationship with TSMC, the world's largest producer of advanced chips. Nvidia's past investments and partnerships allowed it to make the most of a historic opportunity, growing its market capitalization tenfold to more than three trillion dollars in less than two years.

For applied purposes, I later restated the dynamic capabilities framework around three major clusters of high-level capabilities: sensing, seizing, and transforming (Teece, 2007).[7] These are the key groups of activities for organizations and management to undertake to keep the firm competitive.

Other vital operations that support strong dynamic capabilities occur in the course of exercising these three groups of activities. *Innovation*, for example, results from sensing, which includes the identification of new product possibilities; from seizing, which includes the development of new business models; and, less often, from transforming, which can give rise to innovative organizational forms. *Learning* is often triggered by sensing, which includes formal R&D, and also results from seizing, which includes the execution of production plans that can produce cumulative learning effects.

Learning doesn't occur passively. It is a collective process that can improve over time. Failing to grasp learning opportunities is dangerous. An organization that turns a deaf ear to valuable negative customer feedback will soon find itself in trouble. An organization that fails to internalize lessons from alliance partners is wasting opportunities.

The dynamic capabilities concept was devised to capture how Silicon Valley-style firms keep pace in industries undergoing rapid technological change.[8]

---

[7] Although the terminology I use to explicate dynamic capabilities has changed, there is congruence between the superficially distinct descriptions of dynamic capabilities in my 1997 and 2007 articles: "Teece et al. (1997) framed the dynamic capabilities perspective broadly as one of processes-positions-paths, where a firm pursues paths (strategic opportunities) through the use of managerial and organizational processes, shaped by the firm's positions (its existing asset base). Teece (2007) focused on the goal of pursuing strategic opportunities without calling them paths, and then elaborated on the processes for doing so, namely sensing, seizing, and transforming" (Schilke, Songcui, and Helfat, 2018, p. 402).

[8] I sometimes refer to dynamic capabilities as "Silicon Valley management in a bottle." Economics is of little use in understanding the relevant phenomena. As Brian Arthur (2023) pointed out,

Over time, an understanding emerged that sensing, seizing, and transforming capabilities can be engaged to respond to opportunities and threats with innovative new products or an innovative business model. In short, innovation is embedded in, and central to, the dynamic capabilities framework.

2.2 The Capabilities Hierarchy

There are different types of capabilities and different ways they can be classified. Many are technological, like knowing how to build a world-class operating system for mobile phones. Some may be tied to making or marketing a very specific product, such as automobile tires. Other capabilities, such as the ability to offer outstanding customer service, are very generalizable to a variety of products and services.

Over time, I've come to think of three levels of organizational capabilities. At the most visible level are the firm's day-to-day ordinary capabilities for running the business on its current trajectory, which are sometimes called standard operating procedures. These are shaped by a set of mid-level capabilities I call microfoundations. Microfoundations include activities such as evolutionary (non-radical) product innovation, acquisitions, and alliance formation that are performed less frequently than ordinary capabilities but which are vital to help the firm grow. Ordinary and microfoundational capabilities are all governed by high-level dynamic capabilities, which I classify into sensing, seizing, and transforming. The action of (strong) dynamic capabilities is most noticeable when a firm undertakes a strategic change such as shifting its trajectory, changing its resource base, or reshaping the industry. But elements of dynamic capabilities are (or at least should be) always active to some degree.

All firms have sensing, seizing, and transforming capabilities in some form. However, a particular firm might be strong in some type(s) and weak in others. A common example is the firm that is strong in sensing, perhaps through R&D, but unable to seize the opportunities that it uncovers. A well-known case is Xerox, whose PARC research unit invented the graphic display, the computer mouse, and other staples of modern personal computers but utterly failed to turn them into a competitive business.

In special cases, a capability will be rooted in a "signature process" (Gratton and Ghoshal, 2005). Signature processes emerge from a company's heritage, including its prior management choices, certain irreversible investments, and context-specific learning. Because of their deep, enterprise-specific roots,

---

economic descriptors of firm behavior are mostly nouns, such as price, quality, or equilibrium. Understanding technological and organizational change requires verbs, such as sensing, seizing, and transforming.

Dynamic Capabilities and Related Paradigms 11

signature processes are relatively difficult for rivals to imitate. They can't readily be bought (short of buying an entire company).

We now look more closely at each type of capability.

2.2.1 Ordinary and Superordinary Capabilities

Ordinary capabilities, which encompass operations, administration, and governance of the firm's activities, allow the firm to produce and sell a defined (and static) set of products and services. They are what most people think of when they think of what firms do. Although they are mere table stakes when it comes to creating competitive advantage, they can take up enormous amounts of managerial time and effort. However, not everyone understands that while strong ordinary capabilities are necessary for high performance, they are not sufficient.

Ordinary capabilities reside in routines that bring together some combination of (1) skilled personnel, possibly including independent contractors; (2) facilities and equipment; and (3) administrative coordination. These elements are combined into routines that may become honed over time into "best practices" that can be benchmarked against comparable routines in multiple production units within a firm or at rival firms using metrics such as labor productivity, inventory turns, and time per call.

The object of ordinary capabilities is technical efficiency in providing a fixed group of products and services, regardless of how well- or ill-suited the outputs are to the firm's competitive needs (Teece, 2007). When these outputs are well-matched to demand and technology is stable, the development of what might be thought of as "superordinary" capabilities (the "signature process" version of ordinary capabilities) can provide an advantage over rivals. But there is no guarantee that the strong ordinary capabilities needed today will be the right (or even a profitable) path to follow in the future. This determination is the task for the firm's dynamic capabilities.

Superordinary capabilities are rooted in a company's special skills and unique ways of operating. In place of inflexible rules, they evolve through creative learning and problem-solving activities that often involve users. Superordinary capabilities are specific to a single domain, such as internal combustion (but not electric) vehicles or microprocessor (but not memory) integrated circuits. The "Toyota Production System" – a tightly integrated set of processes that encompasses the entire value chain from product design to customer relations (Womack, Jones, and Roos, 1990) – is a classic example. It provided Toyota a source of competitive advantage for decades despite numerous and sustained attempts by rivals at imitation. But such capabilities may not be transferable when circumstances change; Toyota's excellence in sourcing and assembling components for internal combustion engine vehicles may not provide it a strong base for competing in software-heavy electric vehicles powered by lithium-ion batteries.

Moreover, in the long run even signature processes become imitable by others. All ordinary capabilities are potentially replicable by competitors, and this means that they are not a reliable basis for a sustained competitive advantage. In most cases, the knowledge underlying any process that can be benchmarked can also be bought or copied by rivals from a number of sources, including consultants, recent business school graduates, hires with experience at rivals, and even, in some cases, information in the public domain. More recently, artificial intelligence has become a new tool to enable the performance of many ordinary capabilities at a high level (Gernone and Teece, 2024).

This is not to say that all companies in an industry will attain the same level of productivity; in fact, the contrary is nearly always the case (Syverson, 2011). However, if enough companies achieve technical efficiency, the advantages of doing so will normally be competed away. As a consequence, ordinary capabilities provide a weak foundation for competitive advantage.

The ability of most firms in an industry to imitate best practices is especially true over time. In the automobile industry, for example, best practices in manufacturing became more or less universal in the 1990s,[9] undercutting the value they once held for the pioneers of lean manufacturing:

> The operations portion of the automobile business has been thoroughly optimized over many decades, doesn't vary much from one automobile company to another, and can be managed with a focus on repetitive process. It ... requires little in the way of creativity, vision or imagination. Almost all car companies do this very well, and there is little or no competitive advantage to be gained by "trying even harder" in procurement, manufacturing or wholesale. (Lutz, 2011)

Diffusion occurs in all types of ordinary capabilities. Even administrative capabilities such as the multidivisional (M-form) organizational structure that was pioneered by large-scale corporations in the middle of the twentieth century will gradually spread. A study of the petroleum industry (Armour & Teece, 1978) showed that, as the M-form organization became commonplace over a period of about fifteen years, the higher profits that had accrued to its early adopters in the U.S. petroleum industry then dissipated.

---

[9] The rise of electric vehicles is now changing the relevance of many of the ordinary capabilities associated with auto manufacturing. The importance of new skills in software and circuit design has enabled the emergence of new competitors such as Tesla in the United States and China's BYD. See Teece (2019c) and Murmann & Vogt (2023).

Of course, in business, fifteen years is a long time, typically spanning the tenures of two or more CEOs. During such transitions, including the start-up phase of emerging industries, ordinary capabilities can serve as a differentiator. Murmann and Vogt (2023) rated existing and potential competitors in the market for electric vehicles using a set of twenty-six ordinary capabilities and found considerable variation, with no clear capability leader. However, their analysis did not attempt to determine which ordinary capabilities were driving competitive outcomes. As in genetics, observed outcomes are likely the result of multiple, interdependent factors.

Developing an ordinary capability in-house can be counter-productive if it can be outsourced to specialized suppliers that have achieved economies of scale by serving multiple customers. This is especially true when the presence of multiple suppliers ensures that the services will be available at competitive prices. Exceptions exist, such as when the capability is intimately tied to future product development.

There is a limit to the competitive benefit of perfecting ordinary capabilities. A focus on technical efficiency can become an end in itself and stand in the way of innovating new products (Benner and Tushman, 2003). When market demand shifts, there is no benefit to having optimized the production of products for which there are no longer any buyers. As the market shrinks, firms may gain some temporary advantage by pushing down costs, but it's not a path to long-term high performance.

A classic example of an excessive focus on efficiency was the Ford Model T, which was optimized for cost, using standardized parts. Several variants were produced, but all used the same basic platform (Alizon, Shooter, and Simpson, 2009). By 1921, Ford accounted for more than half the cars being sold in the United States (Tedlow, 1988). Then, in 1923, Alfred P. Sloan became the president of General Motors, where he pursued a strategy of product variety, with a different automobile model for each price point. Ford was overdependent on the Model T, and development of the next model (the Model A) started too late. By 1927, General Motors' market share had overtaken Ford's. The Model T was discontinued, and Ford has never since regained its market share supremacy over General Motors.

Empirical research on the effects of process management confirms that technical efficiency is unlikely, in isolation (i.e., controlling for other factors), to lead to strong performance (e.g., Powell, 1995; Samson and Terziovski, 1999). This is not to say that productive efficiency isn't important. A globalized economy with ubiquitous e-commerce offers few places for an inefficient producer to hide. But, as discussed below, dynamic capabilities must determine the best uses of organizational resources. John Chambers, under whose leadership annual revenue at Cisco Systems grew from $70 million in 1995 to more than $40 billion in 2007 (High, 2018), remarked that companies must be willing and ready to "change from doing 'the right thing too long' to 'the next big thing'" (Chambers, 2017).

When the external environment signals the need for change, CEOs face the temptation to sustain the status quo by slashing costs. Some efficiency gains may be justified, but, as noted, no company can cost-cut its way to sustained greatness. Soon after Indra Nooyi became CEO of PepsiCo in 2006, she faced just such a choice and decided to focus on building new capabilities for the future:

> I had a choice. I could have gone pedal to the metal, stripped out costs, delivered strong profit for a few years, and then said adios. But that wouldn't have yielded long-term success. So I articulated a strategy to the board focusing on the portfolio we needed to build, the muscles we needed to strengthen, the capabilities to develop. (Ignatius, 2015, p. 85)

2.2.2 Lower-Order Dynamic Capabilities

Certain activities that some scholars have included within dynamic capabilities come closer to a widely accepted notion of an organizational capability as the "repeated and reliable performance of an activity" (Helfat and Winter, 2011, p. 1244). An influential article by Eisenhardt and Martin (2000) launched a branch of research that equated dynamic capabilities entirely with "simple rules" that would "break down" in the most dynamic business environments, when industries are undergoing formation or transformation. Their approach to dynamic capabilities focused on capabilities that might reconfigure the enterprise in a limited way but are part of ordinary business activity, such as data analytics, product development, or alliance formation. I consider these to be at most fringe dynamic capabilities or lower-order "microfoundations" of dynamic capabilities (Teece, 2018a).

I introduced this category into my framework because some scholars have confusingly equated what I term lower-order capabilities with my original dynamic capabilities concept, which is presented more precisely in the next section. Lower-order dynamic capabilities lack the essential characteristic of dynamic capabilities as I have defined them, namely, their ability to help ensure the organization's future. Instead, they are repeatable processes with near-term goals that the exercise of (higher-order) dynamic capabilities has deemed worth pursuing.

Eisenhardt and Martin (2000) argued that rivals could match a company's microfoundational capabilities either by direct imitation or by developing a different set of routines that accomplish the same thing. This is less likely with the dynamic capabilities discussed in the next section since they are tied to the cognition of individual managers and/or embedded in an organizational culture that's hard for outsiders to observe.

2.2.3 Higher-Order Dynamic Capabilities

The definition of dynamic capabilities in the field's foundational article is "the firm's ability to integrate, build, and reconfigure internal and external competences to address rapidly changing environments" (Teece, Pisano, and Shuen, 1997, p. 516). Whereas strategic management theories, including most of those discussed in Section 4, often take a one-shot view of competitive advantage, a distinctive aspect of dynamic capabilities is that they enable the renewal of strategic advantage as the business environment shifts. This is made possible by top management adopting an entrepreneurial stance. As economist Israel Kirzner observed, entrepreneurs (including entrepreneurial managers) require "the courage and vision necessary to *create* the future in an uncertain world" (Kirzner, 1985, p. 64, italics in the original).

Firms with strong dynamic capabilities may prove able to shape competition and marketplace outcomes through entrepreneurship, innovation, and semi-continuous asset orchestration (Teece, 2007). For instance, industry architectures can be shaped in favorable ways through investments in platform technologies or through technology architecture decisions (Pisano and Teece, 2007). In the 1960s, IBM was able to shape the architecture of the mainframe computer industry with a bold commitment of resources to developing its System/360 family of computers. Other key activities for shaping the business environment include corporate and venture capital investments, and co-investment, with alliance partners.

Responding effectively to (and, in some cases, creating) change requires anticipation and preparation. The organization and its top management must develop conjectures about the evolution of consumer preferences, business problems, and technology; validate and fine-tune them; settle on a means of effectively exploiting them; and then realign assets and activities to bring this about. These are the sensing, seizing, and transforming activities mentioned earlier and are discussed in more detail in Section 3.

The employment of a dynamic capability occasionally hinges almost entirely on the decision of an individual or a team. In most cases, though, dynamic capabilities cannot be precisely located within the enterprise because the managerial component would not be as effective without the organizational elements underlying it. The dynamic capabilities that allow outstanding companies to innovate, maintain profitability, and sustain relevance are diffused throughout the organization and supported by an entrepreneurial culture and significant decentralization. In ordinary companies, some or all of the organizational factors are ignored or taken for granted – with negative consequences – rather than being identified, nurtured, and maintained. All companies perform some level of sensing, seizing, and transforming; they gather information, they make strategy, and they fill out an organization chart. But consciously cultivating these types of activities as part of a creative, entrepreneurial organizational culture can help augment their effectiveness. And viewing them through a system-wide, dynamic-capabilities lens helps to recognize their interdependence and how they can lay the foundation for future success (Grewal and Slotegraaf, 2007).

Deeply embedded enablers of dynamic capabilities are an organization's values and culture, which develop gradually along a path that is unique to each organization. Albert Bourla, the CEO who led Pfizer through its rapid development and ramp of a successful Covid vaccine, had previously transformed the company to improve its agility, positioning it to deliver rapid results during the pandemic:

> We all agreed that the transformation we were driving would only succeed if we had the right culture, and it had to be particular to Pfizer. You can't simply go to Harvard and the best business schools and ask: "Which company has the best culture, so we can copy it?" The winning cultures always should be tailored to the specific needs of the industry in which the company operates, and to the ... challenges and opportunities ahead in the next decade. ... And you also have to take into account the heritage of the company. (Chopoorian and Gross, 2021)

Desirable attributes for an entrepreneurial culture include openness to new ideas and new methods, high levels of trust and engagement, and the willingness to invest boldly and to accept honest failure as part of learning. Also useful is a sense of urgency, including a readiness to see that "good enough" today is generally more valuable than perfection tomorrow.[10]

Because an organization's culture is slow to change, it can be one of the keys (or roadblocks) to a successful transformation when strategic renewal is needed. Cultural change requires wise leadership (Nonaka and Takeuchi, 2011) and should aim to preserve what works with the current strategy rather than to sweep everything away (Katzenbach, Steffen, and Kronley, 2012).

At the level of dynamic capabilities, entrepreneurial mindsets, rules of thumb, and ways of interacting that the top management team has developed over time – its signature processes – can be quite mysterious to outsiders. As Apple CEO Tim Cook said in February 2013 with reference to the company's

---

[10] Urgency should not become continuous or else burnout is likely to result. One approach is to use public deadlines, such as scheduled product launches. These provide a climax which can be followed by a sense of accomplishment and some downtime.

ability to integrate hardware, software, and services: "Apple has the ability to innovate in all three of these spheres and create magic.... This isn't something you can just write a check for. This is something you build over decades" (AFP, 2013).

Because of their deep, enterprise-specific roots, signature processes and entrepreneurial styles are not so easily imitated by rival firms. Other firms will not share the same history and may have a different, incompatible corporate culture. This is true of many, if not most, dynamic capabilities, and their difficulty of imitation by other firms is one reason they can serve (unlike ordinary capabilities) as a source of competitive advantage in the medium to long term. It's also hard for rivals to be sure what factors really account for a firm's success, so they can't even be sure what they ought to be imitating – a situation called "uncertain imitability" (Lippman and Rumelt, 1982).

The most (potentially) flexible component of dynamic capabilities is management. Top management, as it processes the insights and data that the organization has assembled, can decide that the direction of the organization needs to change. This does not mean that change will take place immediately, but it initiates the process of overcoming organizational inertia.

In the dynamic capabilities approach, managers are called on to play more than operational roles (Teece, 2016a). They must develop and nurture an entrepreneurial culture inside the business enterprise and foster relationships with external partners such as suppliers of inputs and providers of complementary products and services. Many team members must be entrepreneurial, identifying opportunities and devising innovative means to pursue them. Others are needed to exercise forward-looking leadership, uniting the organization around a shared vision of the future, which is more important than ever as a growing share of workers operate remotely. Time is always of the essence. The management team must engage in continuous environmental scanning and analysis, asset orchestration, risk calibration, and entrepreneurial action. That said, they still bear responsibility for the operational management required to maintain strong ordinary capabilities. In small firms, especially startups, these different roles may all be taken on by a small team, which generally makes coordination easier. In large enterprises, getting all the elements right is quite a challenge.[11]

---

[11] In the mid-twentieth century, large, diversified firms began to adopt the multidivisional (M-Form) enterprise structure, as explained by Chandler (1977) and Williamson (1975). This pushed operational decisions to the divisions and allowed a central office to focus on strategy. While this is not a perfect concordance with how ordinary and dynamic capabilities should be managed, there are commonalities.

Dynamic capabilities require resources, time, and attention to create and maintain. Some capability development occurs semiautomatically with experience; but deliberate investments in knowledge articulation, such as refining the method by which target firms are identified, acquired, and integrated, are also necessary (Zollo and Winter, 2002).

Entrepreneurial managers, a key resource for capability development, are hard to find. Managers without an entrepreneurial orientation are often not very trainable. Entrepreneurial managers need to keep at least one eye on the future and carve out time to focus on issues such as potential disruptions and emerging technologies from all the time they must spend dealing with current operations and frequent emergencies.

Not every competitive environment necessarily requires strong dynamic capabilities, though. Strong dynamic capabilities are most needed in industries facing deep uncertainty and/or a great deal of technological, regulatory, or geopolitical ferment, forces which have been rising in prominence (Teece, 2022a). While the dynamic capabilities framework was initially developed to capture the way Silicon Valley firms experiment and adjust as they generate and respond to new technologies, it has proved sufficiently flexible to deal with a growing range of challenges.

2.3 Delimiting Dynamic Capabilities

Various scholars have characterized dynamic capabilities differently (Di Stefano, Peteraf, and Verona, 2010). The "simple rules" version proffered by Eisenhardt and Martin (2000) is similar to Winter's approach, which holds that dynamic capabilities are limited to learned behaviors that are at least "quasi-repetitious" (Winter, 2003, p. 991). He contrasts this with what he calls "ad hoc" approaches to change: "Brilliant improvisation is not a routine" (ibid.). Unfortunately, the routine-based approach does considerable violence to the foundational conceptualizations of dynamic capabilities in my 1997 and 2007 articles (Augier and Teece, 2009).

The problem with restricting dynamic capabilities to routines or rules is that it takes the (entrepreneurial) manager out of capabilities, which limits the possibility that capabilities could form the basis of a distinctive competitive advantage. Yet the whole point of the dynamic capabilities concept was to explain the basis of competitive advantage (Teece, Pisano, and Shuen, 1997). The issue was not only that companies needed the ability to reconfigure resources to stay competitive but that they needed the ability to decide when, why, and how to do so (Augier and Teece, 2009).

One way for the routine-based version to link with the Teecian conception was through the creation of the concept of "dynamic managerial capabilities," which focused exclusively on managerial decision making with respect to organizational change (Adner and Helfat, 2003; Helfat and Martin, 2015). This line of research developed separately from the routine-based approach, and the two can be seen as complementary: evolutionary routines govern normal operations, while dynamic managerial capabilities determine the timing and nature of non-evolutionary organizational change.

Winter himself has more recently come closer to embracing a unified, system-based perspective, noting that it was now more a difference in how much emphasis he and I placed on automatic routines versus deliberative decisions (Winter, 2017). Similarly, Eisenhardt has posited the existence of higher dynamic capabilities that govern the addition and subtraction of the simple rules she previously identified as dynamic capabilities (Bingham and Eisenhardt, 2011). There is not any deep contradiction among these approaches; they each encompass the same phenomena but choose to view them through a different lens, be it evolutionary, behavioral, or entrepreneurial. In my view, though, the entrepreneurial lens is the most relevant.

Figure 1 shows a simplified view of the capabilities of the firm, summarizing the discussion so far. At the core are the high-level dynamic capabilities (summarized as sensing, seizing, and transforming) that depend heavily on the cognitive characteristics of entrepreneurial managers.[12] Supporting these are the lower-order (Eisenhardtian) dynamic capabilities, such as alliance formation, that are somewhat more routinized, often with signature processes. For the purposes of exposition, dynamic capabilities are shown (periodically) influencing ordinary capabilities through innovation and learning, although there are other routes such as through flexible organization design, incentive systems, and so on. Ordinary capabilities are the "nuts and bolts," the everyday operations that are necessary but not sufficient to support competitive advantage. They are what companies measure with standard KPIs and what business schools and other trade schools teach students to perform. Examples include manufacturing, finance, and marketing. Any of these can potentially, through learning and invention, become superordinary capabilities that provide differentiation and a source of competitive advantage. To summarize, the figure shows that dynamic capabilities (supported by activities and assets internal and external to the firm) promote and animate innovation and learning. These processes, harnessed as part of management's efforts to maintain the alignment of ordinary and superordinary capabilities with strategy (not shown), drive competitive advantage for the business enterprise. The competitive advantage of the firm, in turn, helps drives dynamic competition and productivity improvements in the economy at large.

---

[12] My students call these "Teecian" dynamic capabilities.

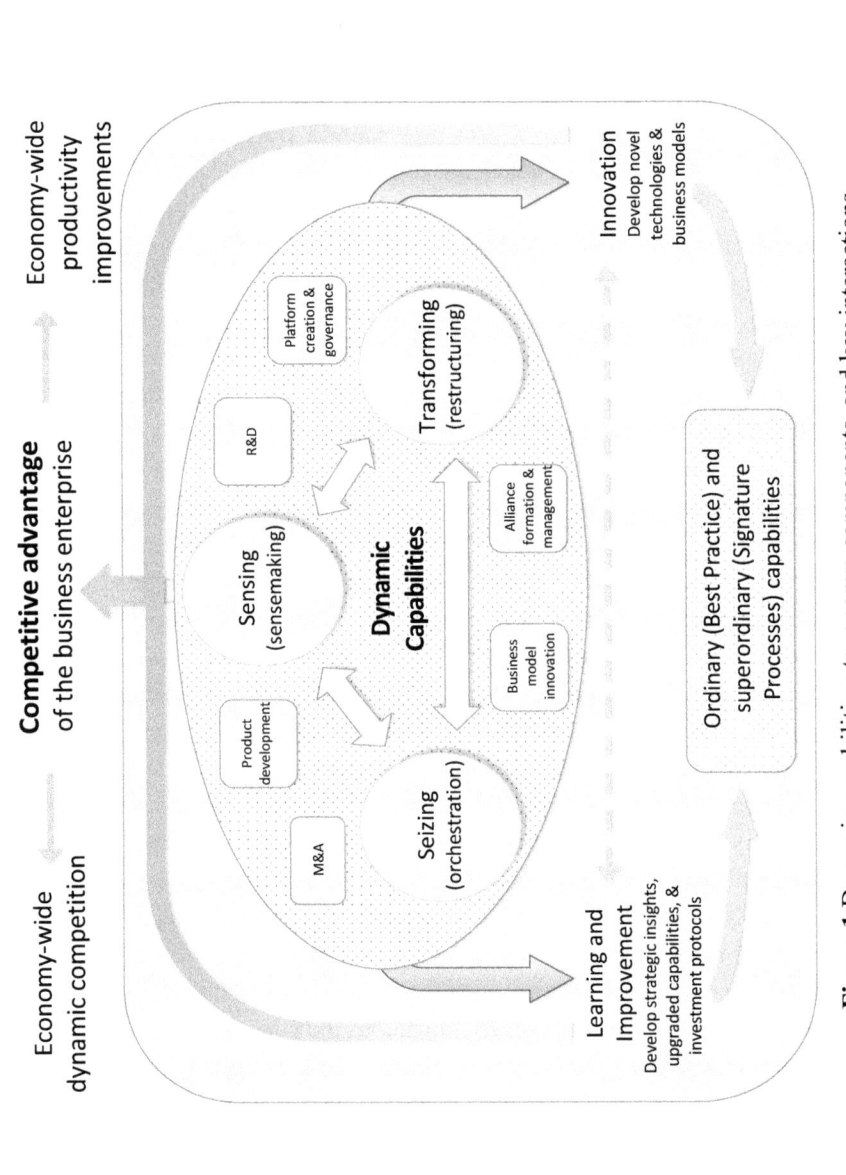

Figure 1 Dynamic capabilities: taxonomy, components, and key interactions

2.4 Strategy

Most definitions of dynamic capabilities separate them from strategy, although they may be somewhat integrated in practice, at least with respect to strategy formulation. Strong dynamic capabilities guide the development of strategies that create and capture value, and they ensure that the strategies are supported by the necessary ordinary (and superordinary) capabilities. In other words, dynamic capabilities and strategy are tightly interdependent, and together they codetermine performance.

Just as capabilities can be weak or strong, all strategy is not what Richard Rumelt (2011) would call "good strategy." In fact, he says that "good strategy is the exception, not the rule" (p.4). For Rumelt, a strategy is "bad" when it fails to define the challenge, fails to identify a path to overcoming the challenge, pursues vague, buzzword-filled goals, or pursues too many objectives at once.

Thus, to be fully effective, strong dynamic capabilities must be exercised in support of a sound strategy. Firms with weaker capabilities will require different strategies from firms with stronger capabilities. And the effectiveness of dynamic capabilities will be compromised by poor strategy. In short, congruence between strategy and capabilities (and business models and organization design) is critical. Much of the literature in organizational behavior that discusses dynamic capabilities leaves out the strategy dimension.

A strategy can be defined as "a coherent set of analyses, concepts, policies, arguments, and actions that respond to a high-stakes challenge" (Rumelt, 2011, p. 6). According to Rumelt (2011), a good strategy has (1) prescient diagnoses that identify obstacles, (2) a guiding policy specifies an approach to overcoming them, and (3) coherent action consists of feasible coordinated activities that implement the policy. A good strategy will often not appear fully formed, but instead emerge over a period of trial and error (provided the business environment is sufficiently forgiving to allow experimentation). New capabilities may need to be developed (if the market opportunity allows). While the actions dictated by the strategy may be visible to rivals and freely imitable, rivals may not perceive it in their interest to do so until it is too late because the underlying diagnosis and policy can be kept secret.

Strategy, when developed successfully, leads to deploying the firm's scarce assets in clever ways that make the most of its resources (including capabilities) and of competitors' vulnerabilities. The goal is to outmaneuver rivals by taking advantage of their weaknesses and mistakes, leveraging in-house and external-partner strengths, and overcoming any constraints imposed by the firm's own legacy assets and customer base.

The story of David and Goliath can be interpreted as one of strategy defeating a rival's strong (ordinary) capability. David couldn't match Goliath's strength but outwitted him with a (strategically) well-placed sling shot.

Strategic analysis includes the identification of promising "isolating mechanisms" that hinder the erosion of profits through imitation by rivals (Rumelt, 1984). There is a range of possibilities, including patents or trade secrets to protect key knowledge assets, switching costs to promote customer lock-in, and rapid scaling to secure large market share and cost advantages before potential rivals can react.

Dynamic capabilities shape the parameters of any potential strategy. Sensing determines the information available for formulating a strategy. Seizing capabilities, such as asset orchestration, determine how complex and demanding a strategy is practicable. Transformation determines the organization's flexibility and the range of capabilities the strategy team has to work with.

Capabilities and strategy are different in kind. Whereas capabilities are organizationally embedded and path-dependent, strategy is more context-specific and transitory (Teece, 2014). Strategy is often associated with a particular CEO, and the median tenure of CEOs in the S&P 500 declined from 6 years in 2013 to 4.8 years in 2022 (Chen, 2023). However, a study of CEO performance suggests that CEOs create the most value after ten years in the job (Citrin, Hildebrand, and Stark, 2019). Moreover, strategy formulation is sometimes a sequential process applied to one problem at a time, while the elements of dynamic capabilities (sensing, seizing, and transforming) are ongoing processes not confined to a single business or technology.

There are, however, similarities. For example, both the firm's level of investment in developing dynamic capabilities and its choice of a strategy should be determined in large part by the degree of predictability of the competitive environment it faces (Reeves, Love, and Tillmanns, 2012; Teece, Peteraf, and Leih, 2016). Greater uncertainty requires stronger dynamic capabilities and more flexible strategies.

The line between dynamic capabilities and strategy is not clear or rigid, and the definitions used by some authors may reflect more overlap than others. With my preferred definitions, there are areas of overlap and integration. When the top management team engages in sensemaking and hypothesis testing, they may arrive at a point that answers a question such as "what new business is the most promising for creating customer value and profit opportunities?" Similarly, the seizing process of recognizing and closing capability gaps responds to the question of "how can this company move most effectively into a new opportunity?" In short, the distinction between dynamic capabilities and strategy is nothing to get hung up on.

3 Dynamic Capabilities

Dynamic capabilities, like ordinary and superordinary capabilities, can be weak or strong or something in between. Strong dynamic capabilities don't guarantee superior financial performance, but they make it more likely.

In this section I take a closer look at the principal categories of dynamic capabilities: sensing, seizing, and transforming. This taxonomy reflects my attempt to distill dynamic capabilities into categories in order to aid implementation (Teece, 2007). These categories should not be thought of as operating in a fixed sequence, although it is convenient to list them in this manner. In actuality, these are groups of processes that should be operating concurrently and more or less continuously.

Research is ongoing to uncover the cognitive roots of dynamic capabilities, principally located in the mindsets of managers. Managerial cognition, also known as "dynamic managerial capabilities," can be mapped onto the three categories of dynamic capabilities: sensing, seizing, and transforming. Each category relies on different cognitive supports (Helfat and Peteraf, 2015). The success of a manager's sensing, for example, rests heavily on the ability to process the stimuli at the core and the periphery of the external environment and to determine where in that environment attention needs to be focused. Seizing will depend in large part on the manager's ability to solve problems (e.g., designing a viable business model), reason through the potential competitive implications of various strategies, and obtain board approval for the budgetary resources needed to make the envisaged investments. Transforming, in turn, relies more on a manager's communication and social skills to inspire trust and cooperation. Hodgkinson and Healey (2011) note that there is also an emotional component to dynamic capabilities, particularly with regard to overcoming an attachment to things as they are – be it a process, a product, or a business model – in order to pursue something new. This mental inertia is just one of the varieties of cognitive bias to which entrepreneurial managers (and company directors) are subject (Thomas 2018). Sensing, for instance, may be limited by the tendency of managers and directors to focus more on threats than on opportunities (Jackson and Dutton, 1988).

The term "cognition" also refers to how an individual stores and structures information, which is sometimes called a mental map or model (Gavetti, 2005). For individual managers, this refers to how they understand causal relationships within the firm, between rival firms, and in the economy more generally. These mental models are a critical element of dynamic managerial capabilities. To take one example, an accurate understanding of in-house capabilities and how they are embedded within the organization is important for seizing a new opportunity in order to identify capability gaps and how to address them.

By the use of surveys and other sources, the cognitive roots of dynamic capabilities can be examined empirically. One recent study (Harvey, 2022) showed linkages between, on the one hand, the narrowness of managerial perspective (detail-oriented or big picture) and organizational design (siloed or collaborative) and, on the other hand, the breadth of team scanning. A team whose manager had a broader perspective and worked in an organization that valued cross-unit knowledge sharing was more likely to scan for opportunities further removed from the industry's current activities. Distant opportunities, in turn, are likely to prove more profitable (on average) than incremental ones because fewer rival firms will search there (Gavetti, 2012).

Harvey's (2022) study demonstrates how the categories of dynamic capabilities mutually reinforce (or undermine) each other. Thus, organizational design (a reflection of transformation) impacts scanning (a type of sensing). But it is also the case that the divisions between sensing, seizing, and transforming (which are each, it should be recalled, categories containing many different activities) are not always as clear in practice as they are on the page. Effective seizing, for example, may require the acquisition of a new business unit, which is logically part of transforming. Sensing can involve hypothesis testing, which may spill into the realm of business model design that is usually described as part of seizing. What matters in practice is the astuteness with which these activities are executed, not their particular theoretical label.

3.1 Sensing (and Sensemaking)

"Sensing" capabilities involve exploring and experimenting with new technological and market possibilities, testing hypotheses about markets, and listening to customers and suppliers through direct engagement, observed behavior, responses to beta releases, focus groups, data analysis, and more. Management must be alert for early signs of changes in consumer needs, in technology trajectories, or in the competitive positioning of other companies that can threaten a firm's existing position or open the possibility of a new or better one. Jeremy Darroch, the former CEO and current chairman of the British media company Sky Group, explained, "We don't spend too much time being overly precise on predicting specific outcomes. We want to understand the trends, take a wide view to make sure that we can see them in the broadest context, and then figure out how to step into them" (Lancefield and Gross, 2020). At the same time, management must be peering further into possible futures as a means of coping with multiple sources of uncertainty in the business environment.

3.1.1 An Alert Organization

In order to sense upcoming transitions effectively, a strong bias for sniffing out potentially useful information must be embedded throughout the organization and its culture, and the organization's design must foster the free flow of information from its collection point to wherever it may be relevant. The flow of information will generally be upward in the organization but should be sideways when it's of obvious relevance to a particular unit or functional area. These flows can be supported by formal processes and incentive systems that encourage collaboration and interaction, but the sharing of information will generally depend on the coherence of social networks within the firm (Becker, 2007).

Valuable information may arise from the application of data analytics to real-time market data, which may reveal an anomaly or pattern that can't be accounted for by management's current mental model of its business. It can also arise from formal processes such as R&D or problem-solving teams assembled to investigate a new challenge from first principles.

The organization-wide sensing in dynamic capabilities is analogous to the concept of "opportunity recognition" by individuals from the entrepreneurship literature (e.g., Baron and Ensley, 2006). In some cases, an entrepreneur may have access to information unavailable to rivals (Kirzner, 1973). In other instances, sensing is a function of managerial insight and vision. The world wasn't clamoring for a coffee house on every corner, but Starbucks, under the guidance of Howard Schultz, recognized and then successfully developed and exploited the potential new market. More often, though, opportunity recognition is a matter of a firm's managers and experts doggedly engaging in established routines, such as continuous research and development, external scanning of technologies and markets, and repeated reviewing and interpreting potential ways to establish a better competitive position. This requires focusing not just on likely scenarios but also on the periphery, such as other industries where incipient competitive threats may be developing (Day and Schoemaker, 2006).

In many cases, particularly those involving externally sourced information, the same facts will also be visible to rivals, but they may assess the facts differently or may process them more slowly. Management teams often find it difficult to look beyond a narrow search horizon tied to established competences. Major firms, such as General Motors and IBM, were able to overcome the problem of becoming trapped in their deeply ingrained assumptions, information filters, and problem-solving strategies, while, for an unlucky few, like Digital Equipment Corporation, these mistakes proved fatal (Henderson, 1994).

When information flows properly, top management will receive a stream of strong and weak signals. Vital capabilities for larger organizations include organizing vast pools of heterogeneous data and conducting effective analysis. An effective implementation of artificial intelligence can simplify this process but must not become a support that weakens management's own ability to analyze signals. The observations that result then need to be prioritized and interpreted to develop a set of scenarios about the future of the firm's business ecosystem.

3.1.2 Making Sense under Uncertainty

A very few predictions, such as Moore's Law for semiconductors (at least for about forty years), or those based on manufacturing learning curves, are fairly certain. By contrast, a high degree of uncertainty pervades most efforts to understand how new technologies (e.g., blockchain, quantum computing, or artificial intelligence) will evolve and eventually be used. The less clear the future, the more management must engage in a process of building and testing (usually informal) hypotheses about the signals it has gathered. By conducting limited experiments with prices, quantities, or features, management can test and refine its conjectures.[13]

This process of sensemaking (i.e., developing an understanding of causes and effects) allows management to build a model of the future ahead of the competition. As economist Kenneth Boulding (1984) remarked, "while we have to be prepared to be surprised by the future, we do not have to be dumbfounded." A firm can prepare for a surprise even if it can't predict its nature with any precision. The goal is to develop a state of mind (and a corporate culture) that does not freeze when crisis hits.

Sensemaking, sometimes called diagnosis (Mintzberg, Raisinghani, and Théorêt, 1976), is never a fixed routine that can be followed precisely. It's more a creative act. The general principle is that of "abductive reasoning," which involves the development of conjectures that might explain patterns in pools of data. Such reasoning can then be used to create hypotheses about the evolution of the business environment (Hanson, 1958, p. 85; Teece, Peteraf, and Leih, 2016). Whereas induction and deduction seek to explain the past, abductive reasoning seeks to develop new ideas, hypotheses, and predictions about the future. An "abduction" is not necessarily logically or scientifically true; firms must undertake formal and informal tests to generate data and

---

[13] Digital platform organizations can often perform real-time experiments and hypothesis testing. This opportunity is available to non-software firms, too. In 2021, Pfizer's CEO described running an experiment with the company's sales representatives: "Some reps are implementing new digital approaches, and then others are implementing the traditional approaches, 100 on each side. And we are measuring to see the satisfaction of the physicians and the satisfaction of the hospital units" (cited in Chopoorian and Gross, 2021).

validate understandings in order to gain confidence in (or to modify) a hypothesis or prediction.

Abductive reasoning can be thought of as building a narrative around how some aspect of a business or a market is evolving, with the goal of generating a new mental framing to better understand possible futures. A mental frame is not just a forecast; it also guides which factors should draw management's attention.

When an existing frame ceases to account for observed facts, it needs to be replaced. A powerful device for constructing a new frame is narrative. Jeff Bezos was known for having Amazon's senior strategy team read multi-page memos rather than look at bullet points or slides because "the narrative structure of a good memo forces better thought and better understanding of what's more important than what, and how things are related" (cited in Stone, 2015).

In short, gathering information is only as useful as the capabilities and processes applied to its analysis. Multiple companies can look at the same facts and data but weigh them differently and arrive at different assessments. Good sensemaking is a form of pattern recognition, and a very tricky one because the "patterns" discernable in a complex, dynamic environment are a movable feast.

3.1.3 Long-Term Sensing

In part because large organizations take time to adjust, sensing must consider not just the next few years but longer periods as well. One way in which this approach can be formalized is scenario planning. Scenario planning is different from "strategic planning," which guides the commitment of resources over a time horizon anywhere from two to ten years (Kaplan and Beinhocker, 2003). Scenario planning, or a less formal version called scenario thinking, attempts to peer farther into the future – as far as twenty-five years ahead.

Looking so far ahead squarely confronts deep uncertainty because of the impossibility of imagining every possible state of the world more than two decades in advance. One way to compensate for what cannot be known is to generate multiple scenarios that differ in how key environmental variables (interest rates, oil prices, geopolitical fortunes, etc.) are allowed to evolve over time. The goal is not to predict the future but to consider how to respond to, or even get ahead of, whichever of a variety of futures eventually materializes (Scoblic, 2020).[14] It's a creative process designed to expand beyond the limitations of the personal experiences of those engaged in it.

---

[14] Superforecasters are a category of analysts who do make predictions, albeit not with perfect accuracy. In contrast to the imagination required for scenario planners, superforecasters are best at inductive reasoning, pattern detection, and cognitive flexibility (Tetlock and Gardner, 2015).

The methodology of scenario planning was developed at think tanks called the Rand Corporation and the Hudson Institute in the 1950s and 60s (Ringland, 1998; Schoemaker, 2022). The first corporation to formally engage in the practice was Royal Dutch/Shell, which credited scenario planning for its ability to anticipate developments such as industry overcapacity (Schoemaker, 2004). It has been used by firms such as IBM and Corning and by various government agencies, including the military.

Scenario planning (or thinking), which is one way to realize the dynamic capabilities imperative to sense "around corners," does not by itself generate a strategy. But it can nudge managers to consider a fuller range of possibilities than those that come most easily to mind. Scenarios must be combined with other management tools, such as real options, to guide management decision making (Cornelius, Van de Putte, and Romani, 2005).

A team-based scenario planning exercise can be used to provide a menu of possibilities for considering how to proceed into an uncertain future. A single manager can be poor at evaluating the accuracy of forecasts because most individuals are prone to fixating on point estimates and linear extrapolations of present trends into the future (Klayman, Soll, González-Vallejo, and Barlas, 1999). Through scenario planning, a group of managers can potentially overcome their individual failings to expand their range of thinking (Schoemaker, 1993, 2004, 2022). This represents an important means of ensuring that events with low probability but high impact are not overlooked when formulating strategy.

Despite its potential value for expanding the managerial choice set, scenario planning/thinking is not widely practiced. It requires committing mindshare and resources to the building of long-term – and somewhat speculative – scenarios, an activity with no obvious near-term payoff. Nevertheless, it remains a potentially powerful tool for addressing the deep technological, geopolitical, and regulatory uncertainty that pervades the global economy.[15]

Scenarios are, in effect, speculative stories about possible futures. A typical scenario-building process gathers inputs from a diverse array of experts, known as a Delphi panel. Insights, such as the possible future values of key variables, can come from consultants, top managers, or key stakeholders. The various understandings are then integrated into a small set of coherent, long-term narratives.

Scenario planning should produce up to four narratives about the future, each one following a different logic about the future rather than just reflecting high/

---

[15] At the time of this writing (June 2023), there is growing tension over the fate of Taiwan. Given the non-zero probability of war in the South China Sea, many corporations, especially those that depend on China for a significant share of their sales (e.g., Volkswagen or Qualcomm) and/or supplies (e.g., Apple), ought to be active users of scenario planning. However, my impression is that militaries around the world make more active use of scenario planning than do private firms.

low variations of key variables (Ogilvy and Schwartz, 2004). The scenarios can then be used to test strategies and stimulate new ideas. The process also eases the replacement of old mental models by providing a choice of possible replacements. Scenarios should be reconsidered every two to three years (Ringland, 1998).

The results of scenario development become the basis for developing a long-term strategic vision of how the firm can expect to achieve fitness with the various future environments that may take shape (Schoemaker, 1992, 2022). The scenarios inform long-term bets about what capabilities are most essential to maintain or develop, where to focus innovation efforts, and what investments are likely to lead to long-term profits rather than a short-term burst.

Classic strategic planning is driven by data. An advantage of scenario planning is that a well-crafted narrative can integrate quantitative and qualitative data that is too complex in its raw form to support effective decision making. The scenario-building process itself can help managers connect and exchange views across functions and departments, deepen understanding of relevant environmental interactions, and provide a boundary around the range of future possibilities to be considered. These processes (formal and informal) are, in many business settings, essential for strong dynamic capabilities.

3.2 Seizing

Once opportunities are sensed and potential threats calibrated, decisions must be made. What is the right timing for the selected response? What is the best way to assemble the financing for the required investment? Large cash balances or the ability to tap external capital provide financial flexibility that aids the exercise of dynamic capabilities. Strong dynamic capabilities are self-reinforcing in that dynamically capable firms will typically have retained earnings and high credibility with investors that make it easier to invest in growth initiatives.

When the elements are aligned for new activities to be undertaken, managers must devise a business model (preferably one that cannot readily be imitated) and a strategy for capturing a meaningful share of value that a new product or service will generate (Teece, 2010a). The boundaries of the firm need to be drawn to avoid (or at least limit) the loss of profits to the owner of any external "bottleneck" asset (Teece, 1986). Then managers must guide the organization through the creation and acquisition of any necessary new knowledge and capabilities.

Strong relationships must also be forged externally with the ecosystem of suppliers, complementors, and customers. One of the ways the young Spotify survived against the onslaught of Apple Music in the 2010s was by creating artist engagement through services such as listener analytics and channels for connecting with fans while constantly improving the technology for listeners to discover music they love (Adner, 2021).

3.2.1 Business Models

There are almost as many definitions of a business model as there are business models. Several studies have listed or compared various definitions and lists of business model components. See for example Zott et al. (2011) and Birkinshaw and Ansari (2015). My own definition is that a business model

> describes the design or architecture of the value creation, delivery, and capture mechanisms [a firm] employs. The essence of a business model is in defining the manner by which the enterprise delivers value to customers, entices customers to pay for value, and converts those payments to profit. (Teece, 2010a, p. 172)

In other words, identifying unmet customer needs, specifying the technology and organization that will address them, and, last but by no means least, capturing value from the activities are important functions of the business model. Although certain Internet-based business models emphasize growth over profits, a business that doesn't devise a means for value capture and profitability will not be in operation very long.

A compact but fairly comprehensive list of components is provided by Schön (2012). His schema is similar to the popular "business model canvas" of Osterwalder and Pigneur (2010) but is further consolidated into three main categories. Slightly adapted, the list is as follows:

- Value Proposition: Product & Service; Customer Needs; Geography
- Revenue Model: Pricing Logic; Channels; Customer Interaction
- Cost Model: Core Assets & Capabilities; Core Activities; Partner Network

The elements of a business model must be internally aligned and coherent (Ritter, 2014). At a minimum, the (ordinary) capabilities of the firm must be able to deliver the planned customer value.

Devising a winning business model is a major challenge, and it is unusual to get all the elements right the first time. A firm's proficiency in business model design is a reflection of the strength of its dynamic capabilities (Teece, 2018b). Like any new product or service, a prospective business model should be tested in a small way and the results used to make adjustments before fully committing. In some cases, it will be necessary to "pivot," that is, switch to a completely different model (Ries, 2011). This is most common in startups. Digital payments processor Paypal started life in 1998 under a different name writing security software for handheld computers (Penenberg, 2012). When that didn't work out, it shifted to an offline digital wallet concept that evolved into money transfer for online purchases.

Management's ability to develop and refine business models is a core microfoundation of the firm's dynamic capabilities. The development of a model is best started from a deep understanding of the customer's predicament rather than from a particular technology in need of a market. In highly competitive developed economies, it is difficult, but by no means impossible, to invent an entirely new business model, such as Uber's reimagining of urban transportation (Teece, 2018b). Most often, the new business model will be a variant or hybrid of models in use elsewhere.

No business model can endure forever. The capacity to detect the need for a business model revamp before it becomes painfully obvious is vital. The willingness and ability to displace the existing business model, around which a certain amount of organizational comfort will have accreted, is also critical.

In the 2000s, the music industry learned an expensive collective lesson about the danger of being slow to understand the speed at which technology can evolve and destroy a successful business model. In the early 1990s, the mp3 standard for music compression emerged and Internet usage began to rise with popular services such as America Online. During that decade, the music industry's revenue, driven by compact disc (CD) sales, rose to what would prove to be its (inflation-adjusted) peak in 1999. That year, however, also saw the release of Napster, peer-to-peer software that facilitated illegal song sharing over the Internet, and complementary applications such as SoundJam that could convert CDs to mp3 files. Meanwhile, broadband connections to the Internet began to spread. The music industry went into a tailspin as first piracy then (after the appearance of the iTunes Music Store in 2003) sales of individual songs undermined its business model of selling entire albums on CD. Its (inflation adjusted) revenue continued to fall through 2014 to less than one-third of the 1999 peak before streaming revenue began to provide a new business model for growth. By that time the "big five" music firms had consolidated into the "big three" (Warner, Universal, and Sony). All the key innovations (music compression, online sales, and streaming) that produced this upheaval came from firms outside the industry, which spent the 1990s looking the other way then wasted the 2000s in a defensive crouch.

3.2.2 Building Capabilities

In the dynamic capabilities framework, the understanding of a competitive situation that results from sensemaking exercises may lead to the decision to offer a new line of products or services. This, in turn, may entail creating new internal or external technological and organizational capabilities or enhancing existing ones (Teece, 2018c). In setting the timing and method of capability development, managers must consider the firm's current knowledge base, the likely future trajectories of technologies and markets, and the firm's ability to learn (Helfat and Raubitschek, 2000).

The development of a new product or service often requires adding (or accessing) capabilities that are not part of the firm's current repertoire. Filling these capability gaps requires learning how to do new things – or at least learning about them, if they are to be outsourced. For example, Panera Bread, a chain of fast casual restaurants, ultimately needed six years to successfully add online ordering capabilities, in part because greater efficiency in one process meant that others, such as kitchen output, were also impacted (Jargon, 2017). According to one of the executives developing the new system, hundreds of small adjustments were needed before the new system could be rolled out chain-wide from its initial prototype restaurant setting.

The identification of capability gaps begins by examining the match between a proposed business model and the firm's existing capabilities. The analysis of existing capabilities needs an objective point of view. Organizational instincts work against this, tending toward the exaggeration of current capabilities. This can lead to launching new lines of business with weak or missing capabilities, followed by a scramble to fix problems on an ad hoc basis.

Capability gaps are of at least three types:

- **Technology gaps:** Much depends on whether the target technology is new to the world or just new to the firm, in which case it can either be developed in-house or acquired. Either way, appropriate experts may need to be hired and an intellectual property strategy developed (Al-Aali and Teece, 2013).
- **Market gaps:** Addressing new market segments requires a deep understanding of customer needs, which have cultural and economic dimensions. The most valuable knowledge about customers comes from interacting with them in multiple market segments. Data analysis is a useful supplement to experiential knowledge.
- **Business model gaps:** A different type of learning is necessary when business is to be done in a new way. For instance, the Internet enabled (and requires) online sales, which forced traditional brick-and-mortar stores to venture into the new techno-business space and run both types of business ambidextrously. Even firms in mature sectors such as oil and gas can find themselves venturing outside their comfort zone to invest in carbon capture or other "green" businesses that sit uneasily with fossil fuel exploration and exploitation.

There is a literature to help understand each of the above gaps in isolation, but little to help understand how to manage all three at once. The business risk associated with closing capability gaps is likely nonlinear with the number and size of gaps to be closed.

Once a gap has been identified and calibrated, the goal is to develop (or acquire and embed) the capability quickly and effectively. These activities are key components of dynamic capabilities.

The principal methods for filling gaps are:

- **Make:** Develop the new capability by selecting and developing people, teams, tools, and processes. There may be no single way to achieve the goal, especially if it's a new-to-the-world capability, and the introduction of *any* new-to-the-firm capability will entail some level of experimentation (Helfat and Peteraf, 2003). The necessary learning takes time and can seldom be accelerated. Management must provide oversight, including metrics and other forms of accountability, to ensure that the capability will meet the goals required by the business model.
- **Buy:** Acquire the new capability by purchasing an existing organization or by hiring key individuals who already possess the required knowhow. This is perhaps the most common option. It seems like a short cut, but often entails unanticipated problems of learning and alignment.
- **Rent:** Add the new capability through more or less temporary alliances, partnerships, and consultant engagements. Many of these arrangements require complex contracting, for which legal skills are a prerequisite. When available, this approach can be a powerful accelerator for capability development, helping to introduce the capability at a high (best-practice) level.

A potential barrier to successful capability development using any of these methods is resistance from within the existing organization. Senior leaders must endorse the new direction, promote the strategic vision that requires it, and provide additional incentives where appropriate. The introduction of new capabilities is likely to run smoother where the organizational culture incorporates a willingness to embrace change. Such a culture is one foundation of strong dynamic capabilities, as will be discussed in the following section on transformation.

Because dynamic capabilities cannot be bought, they must be built. In practice, though, management is often only vaguely aware of the learning that needs to take place. It is not unusual for dynamic capabilities to develop over time, almost by accident. But intentional development is certainly feasible, desirable, and usually necessary.

As new capabilities are brought up, organizational coherence must be preserved. The ability to know how processes and functions will fit together is largely a matter of idiosyncratic (company-specific) experience. True alignment involves mutual understanding and shared goals. Acquiescence ("going along") is shallow and easily abrogated. Employee "buy-in" needs to mean more than grudging acquiescence.

3.3 Transforming

Turbulence in markets and in the world of business generates the need for semicontinuous organizational and managerial transformation. This does not mean change for the sake of change. The unnecessary reconfiguration of assets is likely to prove disruptive with no offsetting benefit. The goal of transformations, whether radical or incremental, should be to maintain internal and external strategic alignment of the organization's knowhow and assets, subject to complex and dynamic cost-benefit considerations.

A common means of introducing change is a merger or acquisition. An acquisition may be designed to deepen the firm's resource base on its existing trajectory or to extend its activities into a new area (Karim and Mitchell, 2000).

An annual capital budgeting process, which in some companies is treated as a means of following existing paths, is another opportunity to undertake transformation. McTaggart, Kontes, and Mankins (1994) laid out four principles to make the most of this process.

1. Use a "zero-based" approach, thinking about the right amount of capital and people for each existing and proposed business, allowing for the uncertainty inherent in investments in unproven technologies such as (in 2024) generative artificial intelligence.
2. Funds should be associated with strategies of which the logic has been updated and reconfirmed; projects should not receive continued funding just because they have been started already when there's no known path on which they'll contribute to the growth of value.
3. The overall capital budget should not be limited in advance because capital can be raised externally if planned businesses promise growth that exceeds the current and projected cost of capital.
4. Acknowledge missteps and move on; business initiatives that are clearly failing to meet their projected targets and have no prospect for improvement should be ended or divested.

The changes that result may be incremental or quite radical. Lovallo et al. (2020) showed that more robust reallocations of financial resources inside the firm resulted in a marked improvement in performance (although a few extreme cases showed there was a point beyond which the benefits declined). Apple's reallocation of resources from its never-released autonomous vehicle technology development to artificial intelligence in February 2024 showed dynamic capabilities at work.

In addition to periodic changes, dynamically capable firms transform themselves in small ways all the time. More importantly, though, they can make more substantial changes relatively quickly when the business juncture demands it (Romanelli and Tushman, 1994). As this suggests, a good start (for an entrepreneur or for a turnaround CEO) is to design a dynamically capable (i.e., a change-ready) organization.

3.3.1 Organizational Design

There is no standard organizational architecture for a dynamically capable firm. More often than not, though, such firms adopt flatter management hierarchies, which is consistent with the requirements of an entrepreneurial culture that devolves considerable operational authority to frontline, customer-facing employees compensated under a high-accountability incentive plan. The organizational design implemented must be adapted to the firm's range of activities and to the leadership style of its top management.

The goal is to build flexible structures and processes that enable the organization to innovate and embrace change. Ireland, Covin, and Kuratko (2009), for example, identify what they call a "pro-entrepreneurship organizational architecture," encompassing a firm's structure, norms, reward systems, and resource set, that can foster entrepreneurship at all levels of the organization. The employees at a firm may or may not be individually inclined to welcome change. What matters is that "together [they] are experienced in the organizational change process" (Overholt, 1997, p. 22). Organizational flexibility must be learned.

While the best approach to designing the organization will vary according to its particular technological and market circumstances, several principles are widely applicable. First, companies can, as noted, become more responsive and innovative by flattening management hierarchies and decentralizing authority over operating decisions.[16] This does not mean, however, that top management should have nothing to do. Good design must guard against an erosion of the centralized control required for strong leadership and for resolving conflicts among different parts of the company, especially when each feels empowered to go its own way in terms of investment, marketing, duplication of services, and so on.

---

[16] See, for example, Malone (2004), Anderson and Brown (2010), and Lee and Edmondson (2017).

To enable strong dynamic capabilities, a company's culture, including its mission, values, and management style, should be entrepreneurial rather than bureaucratic. In practice, this requires ensuring that small, early failures lead to learning rather than blaming (Danneels and Vestal, 2020). Amazon, like most entrepreneurially managed firms, has moved on from a string of failed projects, including a smartphone (Fire Phone), a healthcare joint venture with JP Morgan and Berkshire Hathaway (Haven), and a chain of Amazon-branded pop-up stores where people could see and try Amazon's smart hardware gadgets.

The most innovative organizations are open to thoughtful criticism that forces the holders of the consensus view to sharpen (or, in some cases, abandon) their thinking. An application in manufacturing is Toyota's *Jidoka* system that allows any factory worker to stop a machine, or even the entire assembly line if a problem needs to be fixed (Sugimori et al., 1977). In a more strategic vein, dissent within decision-making teams is needed to ward off groupthink and is most likely to contribute to high-quality decisions when trust and mutual respect are high (Dooley and Fryxell, 1999).

A further requirement of the overall organizational design is congruence, the idea that all the firm's sub-systems should be mutually reinforcing (Nadler and Tushman, 1980). The concept has also been extended to encompass the fit between each organizational component and firm strategy, and between the firm and its business environment (Nadler and Tushman, 1997). However, even if all the firm's internal components fit well together, the organization may fail if the output falls short of customer expectations or the system does not generate a reasonable profit for the firm and its investors.

The dynamic capabilities framework provides guidance for understanding the elements of a business that most need to be congruent. A key concept in this regard is cospecialization, which exists when the value generated by the cospecialized assets used together is much greater than the value of each asset in its next best use (Teece, 1986, 2010b, 2016b).

The opposite of cospecialization is modularity (Karim, 2006). With true modularity, a resource can be replaced in a system by a resource filling a similar role without affecting other elements. Congruence between a modular element and the system is automatic because well-specified interoperability protocols (compatibility standards) make the element easily separable. In capabilities terms, many ordinary capabilities, such as the assembly of electronics goods, are modular and can be outsourced, with proper oversight.

Most critically, governance structures, including the board of directors, must support the ability of management to invest in big and sometimes "gutsy" bets. In 2005, Intel's then-CEO, Paul Otellini, proposed acquiring a graphics chip company called Nvidia, long before the artificial intelligence boom that later made Nvidia a trillion-dollar company. Intel's board, however, reportedly opposed such a deal due to the likely purchase price of $20 billion and Intel's weak record with past mergers (Lohr and Clark, 2024).

The path to greatness is rarely paved with a series of small, incremental investments. A big move is often necessary to forge a fresh growth path, and it will likely be risky, or a competitor would already have made it. This is where "practical wisdom" (Nonaka and Takeuchi, 2011) is needed – at both top management and board levels. The wise leader combines objective understanding with intuition to make judgment calls. A competent, well-resourced board is also needed to contribute to such decision making. Too often, management and boards eschew transformation, perceiving it to be "too risky," when, in fact, a "do nothing" or "do little" strategy incurs greater risk.

3.3.2 Renewing

No matter how successful a firm may be due to its prior investments and characteristics, its fit with the business environment will eventually deteriorate, necessitating some degree of transformation to bring it back into alignment. Lou Gerstner, the CEO who revived IBM in the 1990s, said:

> In anything other than a protected industry, longevity is the capacity to change. ... Remember that the enduring companies we see are not really companies that have lasted for 100 years. They've changed 25 times or 5 times or 4 times over that 100 years, and they aren't the same companies as they were. If they hadn't changed, they wouldn't have survived. (Davis and Dickson, 2014)

The idea that firms are able to undergo periodic strategic renewal and maintain evolutionary fitness over the long haul lies at the core of the dynamic capabilities framework (Teece, 2019a). Agarwal and Helfat (2009: 282) define strategic renewal as "the process, content, and outcome of refreshment or replacement of attributes of an organization that have the potential to substantially affect its long-term prospects." This definition is broad enough to cover the technological, organizational, and managerial aspects of change. The changes undertaken can be incremental or radical, proactive or reactive.

It should be noted that all attempts at transformation must overcome the natural resistance of individuals to shift from the current way of doing things. The status quo biases of people occur because of inertia, habit, convenience, fear, or innate conservatism (Samuelson and Zeckhauser, 1988). Simply being aware that a bias exists is inadequate to surmount it (Kahneman, Lovallo, and Sibony, 2011). It takes leadership – one of the pillars of entrepreneurial management – to overcome these natural tendencies and the numerous other failure modes that efforts to lead major change can fall into (Kotter, 1995). A useful leadership approach is what Beer and Nohria (2000) called "Theory O," encouraging bottom-up participation in repositioning the organization for higher performance.

However, not just employees but also managers can be subject to biases against major changes (Bercovitz, de Figueiredo, and Teece, 1997). Due to bounded rationality, they are likely to favor the certainty of plans that employ the firm's current resource base within their existing cognitive frame. Many managers will also evaluate various possibilities in isolation, failing to recognize the possibilities of pooling risk across multiple initiatives. Unless the firm can institute systems to counteract such biases, it will have weak dynamic capabilities and be at a disadvantage against new entrants that have no commitment to a base of existing assets.

Small changes that enhance efficiency or effectiveness can and should be made regularly, probably influenced by one of the movements that fall under the general heading of "continuous improvement" (Bhuiyan and Baghel, 2005). Such moves may be in the service of greater technical efficiency or cost control. In addition to improving organizational performance, these smaller efforts help to build confidence with regard to larger change efforts, provided that any cost cutting is not done in a way that saps morale (Armenakis, Harris, and Mossholder, 1993).

While cost control is simpler to implement than broader strategic change, it may be a short-sighted approach to addressing weakness in performance. In the nineteenth century, making sailing ships slightly cheaper would not have held off disruption by the emerging steamship technology.

Significant shifts in demand, technology, regulation, factor prices, or other variables beyond the control of management will eventually require the firm to change what it is doing if it is to remain profitable. That is the time to apply the firm's dynamic capabilities to strengthen ordinary capabilities and focus on the right investment priorities. There are, of course, endless examples of firms, such as Kodak, Blockbuster, and America Online, that failed to sense and seize the opportunities and threats in a changing business environment. But other firms, including GE, Siemens, and Nintendo, thrived across decades and multiple changes in leadership by periodically reconfiguring their resource base to exploit the available opportunities.

Radical change is of course costly. Nobel laureate Ken Arrow once noted that, if past commitments to a particular resource base were costlessly reversible, uncertainty would pose no problem for the firm (Arrow, 1973; Teece, 2019a); when the next pandemic or other unforecastable event occurs, the firm could just overhaul its business without penalty. Clearly, this is not how the real world works, apart from (perhaps) small software startups. Yet economic models and some managers effectively treat change as costless. For example, the lean startup model, discussed below, advises firms to pivot quickly when needed, which implicitly assumes that irreversibilities are nonexistent or modest. Most businesses of any size face at least a few decisions that involve a major commitment to tangible or intangible resources – and the acceptance of losses on past investments if some assets are stranded by the shift in strategy.

But dynamically capable firms will sense the need for change, resist the sunk cost fallacy, and develop an effective plan for seizing new possibilities. Whether the initial impulse is to change a product, a business model, a geographic location, or some other aspect of the firm, interdependencies will lead to changes in other organizational components in order to maintain congruence around the revised strategy.

The ability to change is built first and foremost on a willingness to change, to question the assumptions on which the firm's current strategy is based. Old successes can become today's "competency trap" (Levitt and March, 1988; Barnett and Hansen, 1996), and current success can blind management to the threat of disruption (McGrath, 2020). Because disruption can arise at any time, firms must stand *ready* to change when necessary. A readiness to change – and to do so rapidly – requires the entrepreneurial culture that undergirds strong dynamic capabilities. A CEO who is able to make dissenters feel safe expressing their true opinions will enhance the top management team's ability to recognize looming difficulties before the business goes into a tailspin (Nijstad, Berger-Selman, and De Dreu, 2014).

Having sensed the need for change, the key strategic question is then how and what to change. As discussed earlier, this necessitates sensing and sensemaking processes in order to develop a theory of market and technology trends. Time permitting, the theory can be tested and refined. This new understanding can then inform the process of strategy formulation. The new strategy, in turn, provides the basis for organizational transformation.

Once a direction of strategic change is determined, the question of "distance" from current practices is highlighted (Teece, 2019b). As in the case of capability gaps discussed earlier, strategic distance must be considered from technology, market, and business model angles to determine how easy or difficult the changes are likely to be. A strategy calling for big leaps in two or more of these dimensions must be carefully considered and may require a strategic partnership to achieve. And any substantial change in strategy requires appropriate changes in the design of organizational structures and incentives in order to maintain internal alignment, particularly among cospecialized resources.

Sometimes the desired transformation requires adopting technology that isn't available, or that would be too hard to absorb. Failure can result not just because management didn't recognize the need to change but, because the new technology was simply out of reach, at least in the market-determined time frame. This was the fate of vacuum tube manufacturers following the advent of transistors; none of the leading tube brands, such as Westinghouse, RCA, and Sylvania, competed successfully in transistors (Tushman and O'Reilly, 1996).

When change is feasible, speed is often essential, either to gain a first-mover advantage or to avoid ceding ground to a rival. The agility to move fast is costly to develop and maintain, but, in dynamic environments, its absence is even costlier still.

Speed is partly a matter of flexibility, such as maintaining slack in certain resources to permit their rapid deployment. A key underpinning of agility is the use of stronger relational (and hence flexible) contracts with employees. These informal understandings between the firm and its employees rely heavily on the firm's credibility and on the consistency and clarity with which it is exercised (Gibbons and Henderson, 2012). Creating a work environment in which employees (1) care about the competitiveness of their employer, (2) are able to solve minor problems before they fester, and (3) are eager to share insights gleaned from external sources makes the company both more nimble and more productive (Hamel and Prahalad, 1993).

Where such a culture is not yet in place, radical change may need to be implemented as a series of smaller initiatives in order to overcome staff resistance (Stopford and Baden-Fuller, 1994). However, a go-slow approach is only viable where the time lost in doing so doesn't undermine the new strategy.

4 Related Paradigms

There are a number of paradigms (i.e., models or partial models) in strategic management that developed more or less at the same time as dynamic capabilities. Some of these are focused on how organizations innovate and learn, which, in the dynamic capabilities framework, corresponds roughly to sensing. Others are focused on the strategic positioning of the enterprise, which falls into the category of seizing. And two older paradigms take a more system-level view toward the enterprise, which entails transforming activities. Although they are narrower and, hence, less ambitious than the dynamic capabilities framework, each of these paradigms has a life (and literature) of its own.

The discussion that follows is not intended to disparage these other paradigms, which have proved their usefulness in certain business contexts. The

Dynamic Capabilities and Related Paradigms 41

purpose of this section – and of this Element – is to argue that the dynamic capabilities framework is broad enough to embrace and be enriched by aspects of each of them. However, the opposite isn't true; that is, other paradigms are not general enough to incorporate the richness of dynamic capabilities.

A related point is that the dynamic capabilities framework adds value to these other paradigms. An exclusive reliance on one of these narrower approaches would leave managers with blind spots, underprepared to compete in a global economy characterized by technological ferment, digital disruption, financial volatility, and other sources of unforeseeable challenges.

The selection presented here is not intended to be comprehensive. It includes most of the better-known examples, such as "Five Forces," and adds a few less well-known examples that have meaningful overlaps or contrasts with the dynamic capabilities framework. Table 1 provides an overview.

4.1 Innovation-Related Paradigms

I begin by looking at paradigms related to innovation, starting with two models that address knowledge in a somewhat abstract form: Nonaka's SECI spiral and Chesbrough's Open Innovation. These are followed by a pair of models for rapid, iterative prototyping of new products and services: Design Thinking and Lean Startup. The final paradigm takes an organization-wide view of how new product development can be successfully managed alongside an existing line of business: Organizational Ambidexterity.

4.1.1 Knowledge Generation: SECI and Open Innovation

In a broad sense, innovation is an ability to create, combine, and apply new (to the company, if not to the world) knowledge. This ability is also a key foundation of a firm's sensing capabilities. While there are multiple models of knowledge generation, here I consider two complementary approaches: the SECI spiral and open innovation.

One of the leading paradigms of knowledge generation is Nonaka's SECI, named for the four steps on the knowledge spiral: socialization, externalization, combination, and internalization (Nonaka, 1991). These steps describe how the tacit knowledge held by individuals is externalized for sharing and synthesis within a cohesive team (Figure 2). Together, the team develops "new perspectives," which it "crystallizes" into an output (e.g., a product concept) (Nonaka, 1994). Upper management must then screen the output for consistency with corporate strategy and other benchmarks.

At the heart of the SECI process is the conversion of personal knowledge to new, collectively constructed concepts. This is different from codification as

Table 1 Dynamic capabilities and related paradigms

Paradigm	Entrepreneurship	Leadership	Innovation	Deep Uncertainty	Business Models	Sensing	Seizing	Transformation	Strategy Formulation	Agility	Internal or External Focus	Learning	Complements and Ecosystems	Market Structure	Systems Thinking
SECI and Open Innovation		Yes	Yes		Yes	Yes	Yes	Yes	Yes		I/E	Yes	Yes		
Lean Startup and Design Thinking	Yes	Yes	Yes	Yes	Yes	Yes	Yes	Yes		Yes	E	Yes			
Ambidexterity	Yes	Yes	Yes					Yes			I				
Strategic Planning and SWOT				Yes		Yes			Yes		I/E			Yes	
Five Forces							Yes		Yes		E			Yes	
Disruptive Innovation			Yes		Yes	Yes	Yes	Yes	Yes		E			Yes	
Blue Ocean Strategy	Yes	Yes	Yes		Yes	Yes	Yes		Yes		I/E			Yes	
Seven –S		Yes		Yes				Yes	Yes		I	Yes			Yes
Learning Organization	Yes	Yes	Yes			Yes		Yes				Yes			Yes
Dynamic Capabilities	Yes	Yes	Yes	Yes	Yes	Yes	Yes	Yes		Yes	I/E	Yes	Yes	Yes	Yes

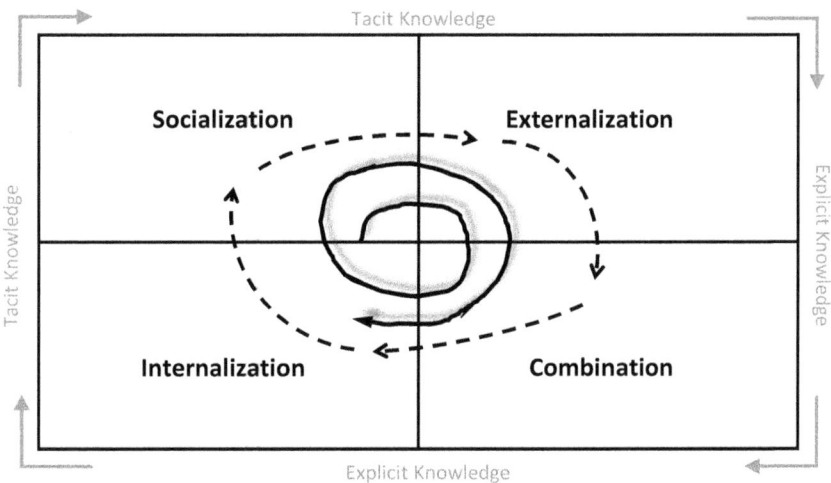

Figure 2 The knowledge spiral
Source: adapted from Nonaka and Takeuchi (1995)

conventionally understood, that is, the simple documentation of personal knowledge. SECI is a spiral in the sense that each collective project also yields new personal knowledge that can become the basis of a new SECI cycle. Nonaka later referred to this as "the dynamic capability to continuously create new knowledge out of existing firm-specific capabilities" (Nonaka, Toyama, and Konno, 2000, p. 6).

A valuable complement to an understanding of SECI is the practice of open innovation (Chesbrough, 2003). This involves the intentional use of external sources of knowledge to accelerate internal innovation. It also calls for the pursuit of new avenues for monetizing that innovation.

SECI is focused on those employed directly by the firm. External knowledge is incorporated through the personal experiences of those involved in knowledge generation. By contrast, open innovation explicitly recognizes the value of knowledge, knowledge creation, and knowledge markets that exist beyond the firm.

During the glory days of large corporate R&D labs – roughly the 1920s to the 1980s – there was both little need and limited opportunity for leading firms to consider collaborative possibilities. Several developments changed this. In the 1960s, shifts in U.S. law made mergers more difficult as a means to access external knowledge. The rise of venture capital funding for startups increased organizational diversity. The gradual dispersion of the sources of knowledge outside the United States, then beyond Europe and Japan, provided further opportunities for collaboration. Rising global competition, in turn, drove a need to innovate faster while reducing the retained earnings that could be plowed back into in-house research.

The elaboration of the open innovation paradigm helped focus attention on the work that needed to be done to maximize the benefits and limit the risks of networked and collaborative development. Firms that had previously eschewed the work of scanning for new technologies beyond their own R&D department now had a template and a rationale for doing so.

The openness of innovation is a matter of degree. There needs to be proprietary, in-house technology in order for there to be a basis for appropriating a share of the value created through collaboration. This is especially important when collaboration encompasses one or more "open-source" networks.

The value capture side of open innovation adds another consideration that a pure focus on SECI-style knowledge generation might overlook. Outward licensing of existing technologies or spinning off peripheral lines of business can provide new sources of revenue and allow managers to focus on core activities, respectively.

The shift to greater openness is not easy or free. Leadership is required to induce engineering teams to remove their "not invented here" blinders (Antons and Piller, 2015). Mechanisms need to be put in place to ensure that lessons learned through collaboration are internalized (Hamel, 1991). And oversight of the firm's alliances, technology portfolio, and intellectual property require greater managerial resources in an open environment.

Open innovation is inherent in dynamic capabilities (Teece, 2020). Lichtenthaler and Lichtenthaler (2009), for example, identified "knowledge management capacity" – the firm's ability to reconfigure and realign capacities for exploring, retaining, and exploiting knowledge both internally and externally – as a dynamic capability that governs the associated sub-processes for open innovation.

The relationship can be seen more clearly by looking at the three main categories of dynamic capabilities. Sensing capabilities are open to external knowledge sources by definition. Open innovation formalizes an important share of these processes. Seizing capabilities can be enhanced by the use of open innovation that creates new capabilities. And the outward emphasis of open innovation on value capture is seizing by definition. Finally, transformation is implicated because opening up the innovation process can allow a redeployment of internal resources away from non-core technologies that can be externally sourced. Organizational structures will also need to be transformed to accommodate inward (value creating) or outward (value capturing) open innovation activities.

4.1.2 Fast Development Cycles: Lean Startup and Design Thinking

In recent years, the heightened pace of innovation in Silicon Valley has elevated rapidity in developing new products and services as a competitive requirement. From its inception, the concept of dynamic capabilities was aligned with environments of "rapid change in technology and market forces" (Teece, Pisano, and Shuen, 1997, p. 512), with the intention that dynamically capable managers would help drive the changes.

In the 2000s, two models of rapid, iterative innovation emerged (primarily) from Silicon Valley. Although initially pitched at software, where repeated prototyping involves relatively low resource commitment, both Lean Startup and Design Thinking have found application well beyond the IT sector. Although Design Thinking includes an initial idea development phase that Lean Startup generally omits, repeated cycles of build-test-learn lie at the heart of both paradigms.

The origins of Design Thinking can be traced to 1969, when the Nobel laureate economist Herbert Simon (1969) described a "science of design" that involved generating alternatives to be tested against the requirements and constraints of the problem being addressed. His approach was tied to the application of logic, contingent on the consideration of possible worlds.

In 1987, an architecture professor, Peter Rowe (1987), noted that designers proceed based on hunches as well as facts. The title of his book, *Design Thinking*, brought the phrase into prominence. Academic research in the design field continued (e.g., Cross, Dorst, and Roozenburg, 1992) with no single definition taking precedence.

Design thinking began to catch on among practitioners thanks to the work of Tim Brown at the design firm IDEO (Brown, 2009), David Kelley of IDEO and Stanford's Plattner Institute of Design (Kelley and Kelley, 2013), and Roger Martin at the Rotman School of Management (Martin, 2009). They saw that the same type of structured, creative approach used for traditional design projects could be applied to many business decisions (Brown and Martin, 2014).

A core concept in design thinking is abduction (discussed earlier), a form of logic that uses "best guess" conjectures to identify potential explanations for facts or potential solutions to a customer's "problem" (Dorst, 2011). The design team's guesses are guided by a frame, that is, a set of assumptions that define the problem and the allowable solutions.

A hallmark of the design thinking approach is its use of an interdisciplinary team of innovators (Kelley and Kelley, 2013). Constructive debate is to be encouraged.

The process to follow is often summarized in five steps: empathize, define, ideate, prototype, and test (d-school, 2010). In less abbreviated form, this begins with gathering project-related information through observation and/or interviews in order to develop a system-level view and to seed the search for novel solutions. Next comes defining the challenge to be addressed, also known as the design space. After that begins the well-known process of brainstorming possible solutions. One tentative approach is then selected for prototyping early versions of a solution, based on which feedback is gathered from stakeholders. These latter steps loop back as many times as necessary for improvement, bouncing between analytic and creative modes of thought. Since this sequence involves bringing an early-version product to market for feedback, this iterative process straddles the (theoretical) line between sensing and seizing.

A key claim is that the use of a structured process helps participants overcome the usual cognitive biases that stymie more atomized innovation efforts (Liedtka, 2018). But that's no guarantee the outcome of a freewheeling design process will be accepted and integrated by the full organization and organizational stakeholders with their own biases (Kupp, 2017). Success in this final (and often unstated) step requires ambidextrous management (discussed next).

While design thinking is obviously applicable to the development of new products and services, the approach can be, and has been, applied companywide (transforming the organization, in dynamic capabilities terms). Instead of a process, it can be treated as a set of principles, including empathy with users, a willingness to experiment, and tolerance for failure, that can serve as the basis for a customer-focused, flexible corporate culture (Kolko, 2015). It has been taken up by a growing number of organizations in fields as diverse as banking, education, software, and healthcare (Fisk, 2017).

The lean startup model bears definite similarities to design thinking, including a call for experimentation and cultural transformation. However, the experiments are supposed to occur *after* the launch of a product, on the theory that customers typically "don't know what they want in advance" (Ries, 2011, p. 49), which means that building empathy with the customer can be omitted (or at least de-emphasized).

In dynamic capabilities terms, the lean startup model was created to deal with deep uncertainty. It is the widespread uncertainty in the global economy (due to technological, geopolitical, and regulatory factors) that requires entrepreneurial management and leadership able to envision and execute upon smart but inherently risky bets. Entrepreneurial management is the key driving force behind creating and maintaining strong dynamic capabilities. While it is a tenet of the dynamic capabilities framework that such leadership is possible in larger companies, it is most often found in startups.

The lean startup model (Ries, 2011, 2017; Blank, 2013) endeavors to put entrepreneurial management in new and established companies on a more rigorous footing. The model enables rapid learning under the deep uncertainty faced by a startup whose leaders may not know yet who their customers are or even what the product will be.

Lean startup was inspired by the "lean" principles of manufacturing. The classic example of lean operations is the Toyota Production System, which emphasized a set of best practices aimed at continuous improvement (Womack, Jones, and Roos, 1990). The improvements in this system tend to be incremental; in Lean Startup, changes to products and business models can be both incremental and radical.

The lean startup model calls for data-driven "validated learning" to inform the refinement or transformation of an early-stage product or business model (Ries, 2011). In the dynamic capabilities framework, this is part of a firm's seizing activities.

The data needed for learning will typically be derived from customer interactions (a type of sensing, in dynamic capabilities terms) occurring from the use of a "minimum viable product" or other form of contact. When the results invalidate a hypothesis, or conjecture, about one of the assumptions underlying a proposed business model, the startup must "pivot" to an alternative, a change that may be more radical than incremental. As the final, validated business model becomes clearer, additional learning is pursued for an ongoing "tuning" process, a continuous improvement cycle called "Build-Measure-Learn" (see Figure 3).

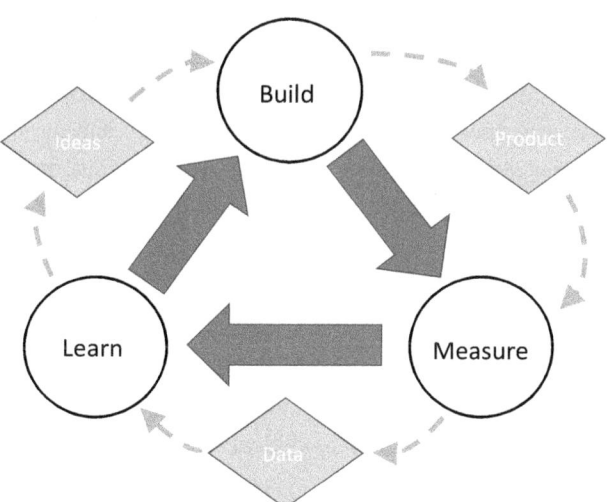

Figure 3 The lean startup's build-measure-learn cycle

A set of core metrics are watched to determine if the learning is moving in the right direction.

Strengths of the lean startup model include its dual emphasis on both developing a product or service and the means of being compensated for delivering it. The lean startup model also incorporates rapid responsiveness and rigorous self-questioning, which are part of design thinking as well. Business model innovation, though, is not explicitly called for as part of a design thinking exercise. Nevertheless, design thinking can be applied to the creation and development of a profitable business model, or a business model concept may emerge across successive rounds of product prototyping.

A related weakness is the lack of an intellectual property strategy (e.g., Al-Aali and Teece, 2013). If the relevant appropriability regime is weak (e.g., in fields where patents aren't issued or are unenforceable), then repeated cycles of experimentation with customers risk revealing key information to rivals before a product has properly launched (Knowledge at Wharton, 2018). Lean startup advocates (e.g., Blank and Dorf, 2020) are also quick to encourage outsourcing of manufacturing or back office activities without first requiring an evaluation of whether such activities are widely available, might represent a strategic bottleneck for the particular product or service, or are intrinsic to the development of future iterations. These and many other value capture considerations are encompassed in the dynamic capabilities framework through the Profiting from Innovation model (Teece, 1986, 2006) and related literature (e.g., De Figueiredo and Teece, 1996).

A weakness specific to the metrics-minded lean startup model is the possibility that its emphasis on validated learning will privilege what can be measured over the pursuit of truly novel ideas (Felin et al., 2020). As in the case of design thinking, there is no guidance in the lean startup model for overcoming the many challenges for organizations that try to integrate and manage the informal organizational structures needed for agile development and the more bureaucratic structures required to run an ongoing business efficiently (Chesbrough and Tucci, 2020). It is to a managerial approach for addressing this issue that I turn next.

4.1.3 Organizational Ambidexterity

The capability to manage old technologies while developing a new one is sometimes referred to as ambidexterity. The dynamic capabilities framework sees this type of internal incubation as critical to a company's ability to sustain its competitive advantage. New business can grow as older businesses carry on and, possibly, decline. Current examples of such dual-track schemes can be found in conventional retail establishments such as Macy's and Target that have tried, with varying degrees of success, to develop e-commerce capabilities.

There is much in common between dynamic capabilities and the literature on ambidexterity. For example, both frameworks recognize that one of the ways to guard against disruption is to develop a potentially disruptive technology in-house that can either match or preempt an entrant.

March (1991) provided a theoretical basis for thinking about the conflicts that tend to arise in attempts to balance exploration of new possibilities and the exploitation of existing business. Organizations operating successfully can come to see their success as tied to specific ways of doing things and other habits of mind that might be dangerous to change, posing a barrier to developing a new line of business that not only requires a new way of thinking but will also draw attention and resources from existing activities (Henderson, 2006). In larger firms, any attempt to adjust the current resource allocation among businesses may upset a delicately balanced set of understandings among division heads.

Tushman and O'Reilly (1996) addressed the challenge, with a focus on how companies could reconcile the potential conflicts. To succeed, the development of new technologies needs senior management support, including access to sufficient resources. The exploratory effort requires the right amount of independence to develop its own culture and incentives while remaining integrated enough to leverage valuable co-specialized assets from the "exploitative" side of the company.

Some of the complications could be avoided by spinning out the innovative activity, forcing/allowing it to attract outside funding and eliminating conflict with the existing business. That approach, however, sacrifices the potential performance benefits of keeping the activities together (He and Wong, 2004).

The concept of the ambidextrous organization (O'Reilly and Tushman, 2004) points to (and helps resolve) the cognitive challenge facing managers when developing innovative new business opportunities ("exploration") while simultaneously trying to maintain existing operations ("exploitation"). Exploration and exploitation require different mindsets. Exploitation is usually based on predictability, efficiency, and the immediate reward of profits. Exploration requires comfort with uncertainty, a willingness to experiment, and patience (including patient capital).

While the organizational challenges of pursuing innovation can be addressed by carving out a space for exploratory activity to have its own rules, structure, and culture, it still needs to be overseen by the same top management team as the company's existing business. Some executives may not see the need to pursue a costly innovation effort and/or worry that their corporate fiefdoms will be threatened by the prospect of innovation.

In order to knit together a truly ambidextrous organization, the top management team needs to be united by a collective vision and appropriate (group-oriented) incentives (Jansen et al., 2008). Transformational leadership is also called for to provide the necessary inspiration (Bass, 1985). Reportedly even Apple has stumbled in this. It created a dedicated artificial intelligence (AI) team in 2018 that worked like a research group with flexible deadlines to improve Siri, Apple's digital assistant. However, the group was poorly integrated with the other software teams at Apple, who pursued their own AI projects. For Siri's ten-year update in 2021 (one year before the earthquake that was ChatGPT), Apple went with the incremental changes developed in its existing businesses rather than the AI team's more ambitious overhaul (Tilley, 2024).

Ambidexterity is itself a capability by which management orchestrates corporate resources across innovation and ongoing (ordinary) activities. Exploration/innovation is a form of sensing, and insulating exploratory activities with the organizational structure requires transformation capabilities. Thus, (strong) ambidexterity helps undergird (strong) dynamic capabilities.

However, ambidexterity differs from dynamic capabilities in that it doesn't (in its basic form) address innovation-related strategic management needs such as external sensing of market potential, designing a profitable business model, or marrying new capabilities to the right strategy. In a later article, O'Reilly and Tushman (2008) explored the links between ambidexterity and the dynamic capabilities framework, providing operational detail for the exercise of dynamic capabilities in an ambidextrous organization.

4.2 Position-Related Paradigms

One of the core issues in strategy has been how the focal firm is positioned in an industry to fend off its rivals. This position is an expression of the firm's (past) seizing activities, but seizing is also concerned with preparing the organization for the future. In this section, I first consider a pair of classic approaches – strategic planning and SWOT analysis – which remain in the toolkit of most managers. Next, I look at another strategy warhorse: Porter's Five Forces model, a structural approach to creating a strong defense. Christensen's Disruptive Innovation model, on the other hand, is about recognizing that the greatest competitive danger may not at first be apparent. And, finally, I look at Blue Ocean, a model that puts the firm back on offense, sparking up new markets in which competitors are scarce.

4.2.1 Strategic Planning and SWOT Analysis

Strategic management as an area of academic study has its roots in the "business policy" course introduced at Harvard Business School in the early twentieth century. Business policy was essentially an integrated form of all the functional skills taught in individual business courses such as finance and accounting. Its application was a form of strategic planning, that is, business-level programs of investment and production. During the 1950s, planning systems were adopted by most leading corporations (Humphrey, 2005).

A typical planning system (e.g., Lorange, 1980) begins with setting overall objectives, then looking more closely at how the available opportunities line up with the organization's existing capabilities. A budget is then developed for investments in new and existing business, including acquisition and divestment as called for. Finally, metrics must be set to gauge progress toward the initial objectives as the plan unfolds.

This is clearly a fairly rigid, long-term approach to managing a firm, and it has its detractors. Tony Hsieh, the founder and former CEO of Zappos, said the world is "going from a mind-set of, 'How do we try to predict, plan, and control and execute on a specific plan?' to a mind-set that's more about, 'How can we get fast feedback loops? How do we constantly sense and respond and build the organization around adaptability and resilience and longevity?'" (Hsieh, 2017). Fast feedback, responsiveness, and resilience are core attributes of strong dynamic capabilities.

Yet planning remains an annual exercise at many firms, with varying degrees of success depending on the commitment of top management, the accuracy of forecasts, and so on. Kaplan and Beinhocker (2003) argued that a good strategic managing process can be a valuable learning exercise that leaves senior managers better prepared for making strategic decisions as the business environment evolves.

An element of planning that also stands alone as a useful exercise for managers is SWOT analysis. SWOT stands for Strengths, Weaknesses, Opportunities, and Threats, the four categories of information to be gathered and analyzed. The method arose out of projects at the consulting firm SRI International in the 1960s that sought to improve systems for corporate planning and change (Humphrey, 2005).

SWOT clearly overlaps with dynamic capabilities. While the analysis of Strengths and Weaknesses is typically limited to assessing the firm's ordinary capabilities, the assessment of Opportunities and Threats is a version of sensing and sensemaking. But SWOT analysis lacks a larger framework to guide the integration of these assessments into a forward-looking approach that allows value capture.

SWOT assessment is part of the second phase of formal planning, which prepares managers to decide where to direct investments during the planning period. The goal is to ensure the fit between the company and its external business environment, highlighting potential mismatches between internal and external factors (Valentin, 2001). However, in many cases it ends up being simply a descriptive exercise that fails to translate into strategic decisions (Hill and Westbrook, 1997).

Along with SWOT analysis, another development in the 1960s was the use of the word "strategy." Initially, "strategy" and "business policy" were used more or less interchangeably, as shown in the title of one of the influential business books of the period, *Corporate Strategy: An Analytic Approach to Business Policy for Growth and Expansion* (Ansoff, 1965; Rumelt, Schendel, and Teece, 1991). Ansoff, a professor at the Carnegie Graduate School of Industrial Administration, noted that strategic decisions are made under conditions of uncertainty ("partial ignorance") and that strategic scanning and analysis needed to be more or less continuous because change had become so rapid following World War II. These elements – uncertainty, continuous scanning, and environmental turbulence – are all vital pieces of the dynamic capabilities framework.

In 1972, a paper presented at the annual Academy of Management meeting called for the study of business policy to be supplemented by the broader concept of strategic management. The authors defined this to include "the process of determining (and maintaining) the relationship of the organization to its environment" (Schendel and Hatten, 1972, p. 9). Other elements encompassed in this broader, multidisciplinary view included the integration of "the sub-parts of the organization" and the determination of "basic organizational purposes" (ibid., p. 11). Unlike the dynamic capabilities framework, which has been applied at levels from top management all the way down to individual managers, strategic management was initially defined as the job of top management alone.

The persistence of planning is potentially a barrier to good strategic management because of the risk that reams of data will blind managers to a wider array of strategic possibilities. Jeff Bezos, founder and former CEO of Amazon, once said that "there are decisions that can be made by analysis ... They're fact-based decisions ... Unfortunately, there's this whole other set of decisions that you can't ultimately boil down to a math problem" (Deutschman, 2004, p. 57). As management scholar Henry Mintzberg (1994) explained, strategic thinking requires intuition and a vision that can attract others to pursue a goal.

Planning has its place. The thoughtful, long-term analysis that goes into planning can inform the strategic thinking of managers, who typically face short-term pressures. But the analytics of planning should not become a substitute for creative strategizing. Planning exercises can then be useful for operationalizing elements of a strategy.

4.2.2 Five Forces

Another top-down approach, and one which found tremendous traction among managers as well as academics, is Michael Porter's "Five Forces" model (Porter, 1980). Porter developed his version of strategy partly in reaction to the SWOT paradigm, which he considered to be unrigorous and ad hoc (Argyres and McGahan, 2002).

The core idea behind Five Forces is that different industries (supposedly) have different levels of profitability because of market structure. This assumption was derived from older competition models of industrial organization economists such as Ed Mason at Harvard and Joe Bain at U.C. Berkeley. They had developed the structure-conduct-performance (S-C-P) paradigm, in which the profitability of an industry arose from the industry's level of market concentration (Mason, 1949; Bain, 1959). For instance, if an industry was dominated by just a few firms with very high market shares, they would engage in tacit – or even explicit – collusion, leading to higher profits. Some economists (e.g., Phillips, 1971; Demsetz, 1973) argued (correctly in my view) that causation ran in the opposite direction: firms that were innovative or more efficient commanded high profits, some of which they could reinvest to garner market share.

Porter looked at the S-C-P paradigm from the point of view of the firms and saw the opportunity for a theory of strategic management. Rather than thinking about questions of competition (antitrust) policy relating to prosecuting or preventing monopolies, he inverted the framework and used it to inform the question of how a firm can create market power. Applying the logic of S-C-P, he argued that, when firms in an industry enjoy or can construct barriers that reduce competition, they will tend to reap high profits. The five forces that a firm must keep in check for continued high profits are (1) new entrants, (2) existing rivals, (3) substitute products, (4) powerful customers, and (5) powerful suppliers. New entry may be limited for technical reasons, such as the large capital requirements of semiconductor manufacturing, or they may be limited by other means, such as the patents that protect pharmaceuticals. Rivalry among existing competitors may be muted if there are a small number of leading firms that recognize the danger of ruinous tit-for-tat attempts to grab more share. Substitute products are harder to protect against since they might come from other industries (e.g., sugar, an agricultural product, can be substituted by artificial sweetener, a chemical product), although in some cases, strategies such as switching costs can provide protection. The other two forces can be suppressed by strategies to limit the relative size of sales to single customers and to multi-source inputs whenever possible.

The Five Forces framework filled a vacuum in business schools and in management consulting, providing a laundry list of factors to analyze as a basis for strategy formulation. It does not, however, help the analyst figure out the characteristics of "good" firms. In particular, Five Forces doesn't account for critical drivers of profitability: the capabilities and innovation of individual firms (Teece, 1984). It cannot explain why some firms in an industry facing a given "five forces" profile are far more efficient than their rivals (e.g., Bloom et al., 2012; Clark and Fujimoto, 1990). Moreover, Rumelt (1991) showed that business units rather than industry effects explained variance in profits among corporations. His finding suggested that company-level "isolating mechanisms" (Rumelt, 1984) or group-level "mobility barriers" (Caves and Porter, 1977) – not industry-wide entry barriers – were most important to understanding firm performance.

The strategic guidance from the Five Forces framework is that managers should somehow pick an attractive industry and further shield the business from competition if possible. This is insufficiently granular. Moreover, it's a static view of competition that says nothing about the strategic necessity to sense and respond to opportunities and threats as technology, the market, and the business environment evolve. Sensing and responding/seizing are, of course, basic to the dynamic capabilities framework.

In regimes of rapid technological change, Five Forces is further compromised by largely ignoring the importance of innovation (Teece, 2007). Whereas Porter considers "coping with competition" to be the essence of strategy formulation (Porter, 1991, p. 11), in dynamic capabilities, the essence of strategy involves selecting and developing technologies and business models that build competitive advantage through assembling and orchestrating difficult-to-replicate assets then shaping the resultant competition.

Furthermore, the Five Forces approach does not consider that innovation typically involves technological and strategic complementarities (Teece, 1984). Integrated ownership of complementary inputs may be required to speed development and/or adoption, which may be inconsistent with the narrow industry focus that Five Forces paradigm favors. For example, automakers are finding that they need to invest in mining operations to secure the key minerals, such as lithium, copper, and nickel, that they need for battery production during the transition to electric vehicles.

Another shortcoming is that Five Forces is not well suited to addressing strategy for platform-based ecosystems (Teece, 2022b). Its industry analysis of powerful suppliers and customers, and its emphasis on the risk of substitution by rivals, leaves little room for positive complementarities among platform users and ecosystem partners. The dynamic capabilities framework, by contrast, can readily be applied to these phenomena (Teece, 2017; Teece et al., 2022). Ecosystem dynamics are seen to be as important as, if not more so than, industry dynamics.

To summarize, the Five Forces framework encourages firms to hide behind entry barriers – creating them if necessary – and hope that tomorrow will look like today. It has provided bad advice for firms and is particularly ill-suited to the digital economy, deflecting attention away from the firm-specific capabilities and complementarities required to succeed. Its uptake and subsequent growth reflected the vacuum that existed in the field of strategic management, along with a thirst for simplicity in the face of complexity. By contrast, the dynamic capabilities framework shows that a firm must maintain a flexible stance, continually search out opportunities, and move adroitly to seize them by assembling capabilities and complements if it is to establish and maintain a competitive advantage over a prolonged period.

4.2.3 Disruptive Innovation

In the dynamic capabilities framework, sensing capabilities are the key to keeping the organization forward-looking. If sensing is weak, the organization is effectively flying blind. No level of cost-saving or process tweaking will save a company providing an unwanted product or service.

A common blind spot is an inability to sense/recognize an emerging competitive threat. Economist Joseph Schumpeter's notion of "creative destruction" (discussed in the companion Element on *Foundational Concepts*) encapsulated how innovations that surpass and displace existing products drive competition and shape outcomes in a capitalist society. In the 1990s, scholars analyzed how incumbents could be dislodged by supply-side innovations that undermined the value of the firm's existing knowledge base (Henderson and Clark, 1990; Anderson and Tushman, 1991). A related demand-side analysis, by Christensen and Bower (1996), showed that, in addition to the risk of being attacked by firms with superior technology, an incumbent can be trapped by a short-sighted focus on serving its largest customers. This could deflect it from competing with an entrant developing a technology that performs worse in ways that matter to major customers but which opens opportunities for some of the incumbent's non-core customers. The danger for the incumbent is that such a "low-end" entrant could be on a technology trajectory that eventually allows it to field a product which serves the incumbent's core customers at a lower price and/or with better features. Christensen initially saw this pattern in the hard disk drive industry, then found it repeated elsewhere. In another example, the market for Silicon Graphics workstations, geared to the needs of Hollywood special effects in films such as Jurassic Park, was undercut when less expensive personal computer hardware and software became "good enough" to perform the same tasks.

Christensen (1997) didn't foresee that potentially disruptive entrants could also begin in a high-end niche, as Tesla did in autos and Apple's iPhone in cellular telecom. Moreover, in the digital realm, disruptive entrants are less likely to be small and uncompetitive. They can just as easily be established and well-financed (McGrath, 2020).

In its more general sense, Christensen's disruption thesis warns against ignoring a new lower-performance but lower-priced product or service, which may appear unattractive to the existing customer base but which appeals to new customers and comes to dominate the industry after it improves over time to surpass the incumbent technology. The theory, captured in the title of Christensen's first book on the subject, *The Innovator's Dilemma* (1997), became popular as an explanation for why incumbents sometimes fail. But the theory's value as a guide for management is questionable since earlier and later studies identified other types of disruption.

The type of disruption matters for strategy. The best response to business model disruption, for example, is not the same as the best one to technological disruption (Markides, 2006). Nor is the required reaction to a higher-priced and higher-performance new entrant the same as that to a lower-priced, lower-performance product.

Christensen's theory is essentially a warning about strategic short-sightedness, an inability of the top management team to sense possible future trends in technologies and markets. As explained earlier, the ability to sense future trends and develop a response lies at the heart of dynamic capabilities.

Clearly some incumbents do demonstrate better foresight. While Kodak failed to foresee that steady improvements in screen resolution would cause free digital viewing to disrupt the position it built in digital printing (Adner, 2021), its main rival in the analog film and photo paper business, Fujifilm, managed the transition period not only by moving into digital print services faster than Kodak but also by diversifying into technologically related businesses in electronics and health care (McGrath, 2013). This case, which has been studied extensively, can reasonably be thought of as a demonstration of stronger dynamic capabilities at Fujifilm. Research is always necessary to determine that a firm's successful transition wasn't, for instance, simply a matter of owning a valuable scarce asset.

Christensen offered some management guidance to incumbents for overcoming the risk of disruption in a book he co-authored entitled *The Innovator's Solution* (Christensen and Raynor, 2003). The solution was a series of rules of thumb, most of which are either part of or consistent with a dynamic capabilities approach. For example, managers are instructed not to use the company's core competence as the boundary for determining what should be handled in-house or outsourced because "what might seem to be a noncore competence today might become an absolutely critical competence to have mastered in a proprietary way in the future" (p.125). In dynamic capabilities, the sensing function addresses the need to be technologically forward-looking to inform boundary choices. Another example is the suggestion that an incumbent allow for strategy to emerge "from managers' responses to problems or opportunities" (p.215) when pursuing innovations that have yet to mature in terms of either technology or business model. The idea of emergent strategy, which dates back to the work of Henry Mintzberg (e.g., Mintzberg and McHugh, 1985), is very consistent with dynamic capabilities, which provide the organization with not only the flexibility to improvise but also the agility to adjust as new information becomes available.

Ironically, the very success of Christensen's core ideas has arguably made them less relevant. Big companies are today very much on the lookout for potential disruptors. It is not, of course, true that all companies are prepared to cannibalize their own revenues by developing an internal competitor for an existing business, but many are. In some cases, an incumbent may try to blunt disruption by buying a smaller rival seen as having the potential to become a future competitive threat. Facebook, for example, acquired Instagram in 2012, perhaps partly because it was afraid that its delay in developing photo sharing capabilities would see it lose market share to the upstart social network (Frier, 2020). However, "killer acquisition" strategies generally don't work as there are often multiple startups aiming at disruption; acquiring one doesn't stop the onslaught.

4.2.4 Blue Ocean Strategy

One of the more recent strategic management frameworks, known as the Blue Ocean strategy, advocates repeated entrepreneurial renewal. This prescription resembles the dynamic capabilities framework's call to pioneer new growth markets as a means of improving the firm's competitive environment.

The Blue Ocean framework emerged in 2005, when two professors at INSEAD, the France-based European Institute of Business Administration, published a book advocating the pursuit of markets where competition is low as a means of earning high profits. Superficially, this sounds like Porter's Five Forces strategy, but the authors, W. Chan Kim and Renée Mauborgne, had something much more strategic and dynamic in mind.

Kim and Mauborgne (2005) described most markets as "red oceans," in which firms compete fiercely for dominance. Success in a red ocean would depend on ordinary capabilities, such as growing scale, introducing minor variants of existing products, and increasing efficiency by cost-cutting; such success is likely to be rapidly undercut by rivals. Crowded markets are also the focus of most strategy teaching. They contrasted this with "blue oceans," markets where rivalry is virtually absent. They pointed out that new markets had emerged frequently in the previous century, and that it was a matter of inventing a new product and/or business model which would allow the innovator to be the first company to profit. This is akin to the notion in dynamic capabilities that managers can shape markets and not just adapt to competitors' moves and the changing business environment. In other words, an innovative product or business model can allow a firm to enjoy a period (of whatever duration rivals require to imitate the innovation) during which it will face less pressure to compete based mainly on price.

As a tool for identifying blue ocean opportunities, they proposed a "strategy canvas" that examines the factors on which firms in the existing industry compete and the amount of consumer value each one provides. From there, the strategist can consider whether any dimensions are excessive or entirely unnecessary (for a cost-reducing strategy), and whether one or more dimensions could be profitably augmented or added (a value creation strategy). They argue that all of these strategies allow the focal firm to break out of the prevailing industry logic into fresh waters. However, some of these strategies are clearly more imitable by rivals than others.

In the case of truly innovative strategies, the Profiting From Innovation model (Teece, 1986, 2006, and the companion Element to this one) shows some of the pitfalls that can prevent an industry pioneer from reaping the full rewards for its innovation, such as weak intellectual property rights. Unless the innovator is able to enjoy entry barriers of the type discussed by Porter and others (e.g., Rumelt, 1984), a likely outcome in most cases is that a first-mover advantage will prove short-lived, requiring repeated "blue ocean" innovations to sustain profitability (Burke, Van Stel, and Thurik, 2016). For their part, Kim and Mauborgne (2005) are skeptical that any company can be "perpetually excellent" (p.12); they argue instead that any company can make the kind of strategic move that opens up a blue ocean market. Strong dynamic capabilities will improve a firm's chances of consistently identifying and exploiting blue ocean opportunities.

A notable feature of the Blue Ocean strategy model is that it doesn't neglect implementation, which occupies one of the three sections of their initial book. The authors focus first on the leadership needed to overcome attachment to the status quo, to build motivation, and ensure adequate resources for the new strategy. Then they address the need to ensure alignment of all employees with the new strategy. These elements are, of course, very much part of the entrepreneurial management and organizational alignment called for in the dynamic capabilities framework under the rubric of seizing.

4.3 Organization-Related Paradigms

In this last section, I look at two older models that take a more system-level view of the firm. This involves organizational design, which in turn involves the firm's transformation capabilities. The older of these two models, the Seven-S framework, advocates (similarly to dynamic capabilities) an integrated view of the firm's competences and their alignment with strategy. The other model, Peter Senge's Learning Organization, is more focused on the organization's ability to generate and implement new ideas. In that way, it shares the forward-looking emphasis of the dynamic capabilities framework.

4.3.1 Seven-S

Five Forces, discussed above, is an example of a relatively simple set of guidelines for strategy that avoids consideration of the internal processes and choices that would inevitably be involved in any strategic shift. The Seven-S framework takes a more holistic and dynamic approach to strategic management, identifying a set of inter-related features that characterize an organization's activities and that must be kept in alignment as the firm evolves. It was developed by two McKinsey & Co. consultants and was popularized in a 1982 book called *In Search of Excellence* (Peters and Waterman, 1982).

Weakness in any of the seven interdependent categories will undermine the overall performance of the organization. The categories are as follows:

1. **Structure:** how decision making and accountability are organized, including the degree of centralization, number of levels of management, and whether the major administrative divisions are by function or by product.

2. **Strategy:** how the company plans to maintain or improve its competitive position by means such as creating unique value, customer lock-in, or acquiring key assets.
3. **Systems:** how day-to-day business is done, including budgeting, human resources, and new product development.
4. **Skills:** capabilities, such as manufacturing or marketing, that the organization performs well.
5. **Style:** the explicit and implicit messages given by top management about priorities, including what and who is important.
6. **Staff:** how managers are identified and developed.
7. **Shared Values:** the sense of a common goal, such as making money or improving the world in some way.

Because the framework makes no claims about causal linkages among the seven elements, there is very little theoretical or empirical research about it. There are, however, a large number of applied case studies demonstrating the use of the framework in a variety of for-profit and non-profit settings.

A similar model, which did include causal flows, was introduced in an article by Nadler and Tushman (1977). In their model of the firm, inputs of environment, history, and resources are transformed, under the guidance of strategy, by people, structures, and processes into various types of outcomes at individual, group, and organizational levels. A key message was that the need for congruence between all these elements had to be balanced with the risk of rigidity that would render organizational change difficult (Nadler and Tushman, 1989).

Such practice-based models have paved the way for more theory-based approaches such as the dynamic capabilities framework, which also calls for internal and external alignment. In fact, the original Seven-S article includes a description of its goals that reads more like a description of dynamic capabilities than of the Seven-S framework:

> Somewhat to our surprise, senior executives in the top-performing companies that we interviewed were concerned that the inherent limitations of structural approaches could render their companies insensitive to an unstable business environment marked by rapidly changing threats and opportunities ... Their organizations, they said, had to learn how to build capabilities for rapid and flexible response ... Their task, as they saw it, was largely one of preserving internal stability while adroitly guiding the organization's responses to fast-paced external change. (Waterman, Peters, and Phillips, 1980, p. 16)

These models marked a major advance in strategic management frameworks in that they build on a base of systems theory, capturing more of the complexity that real-world managers must address. In dynamic capabilities terms, the area where they most fall short is seizing, because they don't look beyond value creation to value capture. In particular, they lack any reference to business models. A business model defines the architecture of a business, specifying the value proposition to the customer and how the delivery of value is to be monetized (Teece, 2010a). Even if all internal components fit well together, the organization may fail if its business model is misspecified and doesn't yield a steady stream of profits.

The dynamic capabilities framework also differs from these earlier system-level approaches by distinguishing between ordinary, superordinary, and dynamic capabilities, which Seven-S treats as equivalent. Seven-S also ignores issues of firm boundaries. For example, ordinary capabilities that are not cospecialized with other resources in the company may be outsourced, reducing the number of elements that must be kept in congruence. The dynamic capabilities framework is also more aware of which facets of the organization and its wider context determine advantage, such as the imitability of company resources and the appropriability environment for its technologies (Teece, 2006).

4.3.2 Learning Organization

Lean startup and dynamic capabilities conceive of firms small and large as flexible organizations guided by entrepreneurial leaders. A paradigm that explores the possible contradictions within these archetypes is the "learning organization," a concept closely associated with Peter Senge, a senior lecturer at MIT's Sloan School of Management. Senge adopted a system-level approach to general management that has been embraced by many practitioners since the publication of the first edition of his book *The Fifth Discipline* in 1990.

Systems thinking is the "fifth discipline" of his title. The other four disciplines are *personal mastery*, without which organization-level learning is not possible; the ability to scrutinize one's own *mental model* of the (business) world and question its assumptions; the propagation of a *shared vision*, so that participants want to contribute; and *team learning*, the constructive mutual exchange of ideas.

Senge's "basic definition" of a learning organization is one "that is continually expanding its capacity to create its future" (2006, p. 14). His framework is thus entrepreneurial and forward-looking in much the same way as dynamic capabilities. He also names "generative learning ... that enhances our capacity to create" as a key capability. Generative learning is related to "double-loop learning," in which a team is not simply addressing a problem but also willing to examine the basic assumptions behind current solutions (Argyris, 1976). In dynamic capabilities, terms, this is part of the firm's sensing capabilities.

Another commonality is the uniqueness of each (learning) organization. "It's not sufficient to copy the approaches used by firms heralded as learning organizations ... Companies must discover their own solutions, not borrow them" (Redding, 1997, p. 62). In other words, there's no simple recipe to follow to have organization-wide learning – or strong dynamic capabilities.

One place where the learning organization and dynamic capabilities frameworks differ somewhat is the role of management. The learning organization approach emphasizes the need for leaders who foster collective learning, rejecting the idea of heroic leaders making key decisions, which he dismisses as "individualistic and nonsystemic" (Senge, 1990, p. 8). The dynamic capabilities approach sees the need for both types of leadership. Learning produces perspectives and options, but eventually decisions need to be made and resources committed.

Senge sees the complex, systemic nature of organizations as a constraint on managerial decision making. One of his key concepts is the "balancing loop" (Senge, 2006, p. 86) by which the system maintains itself in balance. An action taken on the system may be followed by a delay before the system responds. If this delay is not understood, then further action may lead to the system overshooting its desired state and needing to be adjusted backward. As a consequence, aggressive management is likely to be frustrated as encapsulated by one of his "laws": "Faster is slower" (Senge, 2006, p. 62). In the dynamic capabilities framework, the constraints of path dependence are acknowledged, but so is the need for speed when internal or external conditions demand it. And those conditions are becoming prevalent. In 2017, Doug McMillon, the CEO of Walmart, said, "Once upon a time a company like ours might have made big strategic choices on an annual or quarterly cycle. Today strategy is daily" (Ignatius, 2017, p. 99).

In some cases, the creation of a sense of crisis (or the advent of a real one) can bring about rapid change. Another way to reduce barriers to transformation is to invest the effort to prepare the organization's structure and culture to be flexible before change is required.

The mostly unspoken assumption behind the learning organization, much like Nonaka's SECI model, is that constructing this integrated knowledge-generating machine will inevitably lead to organizational success. In reality, it is a theory of value creation without any specificity about value capture through business model design, ecosystem management, or strategy. Accordingly, it is drastically incomplete.

5 Conclusions

This Element presents the dynamic capabilities framework and then compares and contrasts it with a series of related paradigms of innovation and strategy, as summarized in Table 1. As explained earlier, the dynamic capabilities framework is more comprehensive than other system-level paradigms, such as Seven-S, and encompasses the more limited ones, such as Design Thinking.

While the dynamic capabilities framework has built on antecedents, it is a clear break from, and in part a reaction to, more static approaches to strategic management, such as Porter's Five Forces, which in some cases still populate business school curricula and impact practice. The shortcomings of Five Forces were clear from the beginning to anyone who had studied and thought about the industrial organization structure-conduct-performance framework (Teece, 1984). It has nevertheless taken years to wean scholars and practitioners away from it. The glaring omissions of technological innovation, entrepreneurship, and complementary assets made it starkly apparent that what I call the (market) structure approach to strategy was, from the very beginning, not just outmoded but deceptive inasmuch as it deflected attention away from what matters most for the competitive advantage of the business enterprise. The emergence of the digital economy, multisided platforms, and markets where ecosystems are significant phenomena has only amplified concerns about older paradigms.

Clearly, a framework has long been needed that brings innovation and entrepreneurial management to the fore. Any framework that fails to do so is not fit for purpose. A theory of capabilities and their development has been needed to clarify what makes each firm unique and how management matters. Capabilities are inert without the entrepreneurial spark that sets learning processes in motion. These learning processes in turn lead to the development of capabilities. Capabilities (particularly strong dynamic capabilities) are essential to building and maintaining competitive advantage.

The dynamic capabilities framework has given rise to a large and growing body of research in strategic management. It is also starting to have an impact in other fields, such as competition policy (e.g., Teece, 2023) and economic development (e.g., Mazzucato, Qobo, and Kattel, 2022).

With hindsight, it is remarkable that not only the field of economics but also, in large measure, the field of (strategic) management travelled as far as they have without a theory of organizational and technological capabilities. The SWOT framework, from half a century ago, in which the strengths and weaknesses dimensions implicitly invoke capabilities, could have evolved into a theory of capabilities, but that never occurred. In fact, what is striking about all the related concepts and paradigms is that none of them (with the possible exception of Seven-S) dared to address capabilities, despite their obvious importance. Not that it is simple to do so; perhaps their complexity helps explain the lack of scholarship on capabilities in the last century. Moreover, narrow academic specialization meant that few were willing or motivated to flag this deficiency and attempt to address it. Most economists, for example, have a methodological bias that effectively shuts the door on the study of capabilities. As Nobel laureate George Akerlof has explained, economics favors "hardness" (formal models) over relevance (Akerlof, 2020).[17]

Perhaps this is a corollary to seventy years of post-World War II peace. In times of war, business and national capabilities come to the fore. During World War II, friend and foe could see that US industrial capabilities were an enabler of the Allied victory. It was not just a matter of greater resources. After the end of the Cold War, Russian enterprises had access to great resources; but they were hampered by limited capabilities. As "decoupling" from China is considered, technological and organizational capabilities rush to the fore. Executives and policy makers flounder without a framework that highlights and differentiates ordinary, superordinary, and dynamic capabilities.

Perhaps the most iconic entrepreneur at the present time is Elon Musk. The technological and commercial progress of electric vehicles and reusable rockets is virtually inconceivable without him at the helm of Tesla and Space Exploration Technologies (SpaceX), respectively. His ambitious goal-setting and willingness to risk all his own money multiple times have inspired others. Notwithstanding, there are too few entrepreneurs of his caliber – almost none outside the United States and China.

It was SpaceX's high R&D expenditures, quick mastery of rocket propulsion and guidance technologies, and commitment to the development of reusability that were foundational to the low cost per launch provided by the Falcon family of rockets. Because of the lack of qualified suppliers suited to its low-cost strategy, SpaceX vertically integrated – much like Henry Ford did in order to make the mass-market Model T car a reality – with Musk harnessing emerging technologies such as additive manufacturing to produce parts that might not even be possible with conventional manufacturing. In 2012, just ten years after its founding, SpaceX became the first commercial company to send a vehicle to the International Space Station. While providing launch services to NASA and others is core to its business model, the company has also pursued other types of customers, launching a network of satellites that allow it to provide the Starlink

---

[17] Moreover, as described earlier, economic analysis is all about nouns. It ignores dynamic processes such as sensing, seizing, and transforming not because they are unimportant but because they are too hard to model. The consequence is economic theories of the firm with little practical relevance.

internet service to areas without broadband access, including deserts and oceans. This proved vital to Ukraine in its defense against Russia's invasion in 2022. Starlink also provides low-cost Internet service to private and commercial ocean-going vessels.

The SpaceX story is hard to squeeze into a Five Forces analysis. In retrospect, it appears that the firm has created Rumeltian isolating mechanisms (inimitable, firm-specific differentiators) by building unique capabilities, but a prospective analysis in 2002 wouldn't have revealed how to go about it – or even that aerospace was a field ripe for new entry. The dynamic capabilities framework recognizes that there are no impossible goals given the right combination of assets, entrepreneurial vision, and leadership.[18]

There is of course a similar startup company; two years before the start of SpaceX, Blue Origin was founded by former Amazon CEO Jeff Bezos. Blue Origin, which kept its activities secret for its first fifteen years, achieved proof of reusability a month before SpaceX, but it has, to date, completed far fewer launches and has restricted itself mostly to suborbital flights aimed at space tourism, although it also has the moon in its plans. The race isn't finished, but so far it looks as though Musk's aggressive agenda and willingness to fail publicly have carried the day. Paradigms such as Lean Startup, Learning Organization, or Disruptive Innovation can explain aspects of the business histories of SpaceX and Blue Origin, but the more comprehensive dynamic capabilities framework, in which they are all subsumed, is really needed to understand the cases holistically.

Of course, broad inclusiveness is not the hallmark of a good theory. A theory should be parsimonious, stripped down to the key elements. As explained in the Introduction, "dynamic capabilities" is a framework that defines variables from which parsimonious theories can be generated. As discussed earlier, the framework is a practical application of general systems thinking that can enable practitioners to achieve a whole-of-company alignment and to thrive despite the vicissitudes of a business environment characterized by deep uncertainty. As I've said for decades (see also Helfat and Peteraf, 2009), understanding the foundations of firm-level competitive advantage is the Holy Grail not only of strategic management scholars but of investors in stocks and bonds. Policy makers and national leaders also pay attention because the success of an

---

[18] In 2013 (two years before SpaceX proved it could successfully land a first stage for reuse), a revealing exchange took place at a satellite industry forum. There, a representative for Europe's commercial launch service, Arianespace, dismissed a question about SpaceX's reusability plans by arguing that the startup "seems to be selling a dream" (Berger, 2024). As of 2024, Arianespace is not expecting to achieve reusability (and hence price parity with SpaceX) in its launch offering until sometime in the 2030s. Musk and SpaceX have dynamic capabilities par excellence. The European Space Agency (and NASA in the United States) does not.

economy depends on the performance of the businesses active in it. The dynamic capabilities framework abstracts from reality, as it inevitably must, but not so much that it is irrelevant to the issues of the moment, such as how advances in artificial intelligence will impact strategy development and competitive outcomes for particular businesses.

The related paradigms analyzed in this Element are systems of thought that harbor some similar ideas to various components of the dynamic capabilities framework. In each case, I pointed out differences as well as similarities to the dynamic capabilities perspective. Some of the related paradigms (lean startup, ambidexterity, SECI, et alia) address innovation (value creation) but stop well short of value capture. Others, such as Five Forces, focus on value capture but have nothing to say about technological and organizational capabilities.

This Element was created to fill a gap in the teaching and dissemination of strategic management theories. It is rare in the field of strategy that a scholar or a practitioner seeks to systematically relate a focal paradigm to others, except in a most cursory way. Too many business books tout a single theory with no reference to other, overlapping theories. The constant multiplication of concepts has confused managers and stunted the intellectual progress of the strategy field. I have tried to connect the dots here, using dynamic capabilities as a portmanteau, to assist the reader in seeing the forest as well as the trees.[19]

A major challenge that remains is to move beyond the "what" of describing dynamic capabilities to the "how" of their implementation. How can managers build ordinary, superordinary, and dynamic capabilities, then maintain their business relevance over time? The work has been engaged (e.g., Schoemaker, Heaton, and Teece, 2018; Teece, Raspin, and Cox, 2020), but capabilities remain under-researched, both empirically and conceptually.

Finally, my treatment of dynamic capabilities does not distinguish between digital platforms and other types of business. Platforms certainly have some distinctive features, such as their centrality to digital ecosystems made up of complementors and users. However, the dynamic capabilities framework is sufficiently general to encompass the key features of platforms and of the

---

[19] The author apologizes for perhaps overusing American examples. China also has many examples of firms with strong dynamic capabilities. The European capabilities landscape is not as rich as it ought to be. I believe Europe needs stronger dynamic capabilities to become more competitive. This is a longstanding problem. In the 1960s, a French journalist, Jean-Jacques Servan-Schreiber, wrote that "What threatens to crush us today is not a torrent of riches, but a more intelligent use of skills" (Servan-Schreiber, 1968, p. 29). He worried that Europe lacked "the ability to transform an idea into reality through the industrial process; the talent for coordinating skills and making rigid organizations susceptible to change" (Servan-Schreiber, 1968, p. 46). In other words, he worried that European firms had much weaker dynamic capabilities than the US-based multinational enterprises competing in Europe.

n-sided markets they enable. Like other organizations, platform leaders must proactively sense, seize, and transform in order to stay competitive.

Even large digital platforms like Meta, Google, Apple, Amazon, and Microsoft are not guaranteed ongoing success. First off, these firms compete against each other with colossal force, spending tens of billions of dollars each year on R&D and capital investment to gain and retain an advantage (Teece, 2025). Moreover, new, well-financed entrants can appear and scale rapidly, challenging pieces of the established platforms. OpenAI, for example, was founded in 2015 with $1 billion in backing from its founders. After releasing a series of increasingly sophisticated natural-language "Chat" models, it released SearchGPT in 2024, positioning itself credibly as a rival to Google and other search engines by offering a conversational interface for web searches.

Artificial intelligence (AI) can also be analyzed within the dynamic capabilities framework. Gernone and Teece (2024) explain how AI can already significantly support ordinary and superordinary capabilities. As the technology advances, AI will become increasingly important for dynamic capabilities, but key strategic decisions will require human involvement for the foreseeable future.

The dynamic capabilities framework is designed to be useful both to practitioners and to scholars. It guides managers to maintain total alignment across the firm and to look forward to where the firm should be in another five to ten years. Inasmuch as managers receive (often unhelpful) advice on how to do everything better, this framework can help the top management team set priorities. For scholars, it can help reconnect their research to issues that really matter and provide a matrix for professors to help students see the field holistically. The goal of this Element has been to provide greater clarity in these endeavors.

References

Adner, R. (2021). *Winning the Right Game: How to Disrupt, Defend, and Deliver in a Changing World.* Cambridge, MA: MIT Press.

Adner, R., & Helfat, C. E. (2003). Corporate effects and dynamic managerial capabilities. *Strategic Management Journal, 24*(10), 1011–1025.

AFP (2013). Apple still has "magic," innovation, says CEO Cook. *afp.com.* www.globalpost.com/dispatch/news/afp/130212/apple-still-has-magic-innovation-says-ceo-cook-0 (accessed May 28, 2015).

Agarwal, R., & Helfat, C. E. (2009). Strategic renewal of organizations. *Organization Science, 20*(2), 281–293.

Akerlof, G. A. (2020). Sins of omission and the practice of economics. *Journal of Economic Literature, 58*(2), 405–418.

Al-Aali, A. Y., & Teece, D. J. (2013). Towards the (strategic) management of intellectual property: Retrospective and prospective. *California Management Review, 55*(4), 15–30.

Alizon, F., Shooter, S. B., & Simpson, T. W. (2009). Henry Ford and the Model T: lessons for product platforming and mass customization. *Design Studies, 30*(5), 588–605.

Anderson, C., & Brown, C. E. (2010). The functions and dysfunctions of hierarchy. *Research in Organizational Behavior, 30*, 55–89.

Anderson, P., & Tushman, M. L. (1991). Managing through cycles of technological change. *Research-Technology Management, 34*(3), 26–31.

Ansoff, H. I. (1965). *Corporate Strategy: An Analytic Approach to Business Policy for Growth and Expansion.* New York: McGraw-Hill.

Antons, D., & Piller, F. T. (2015). Opening the black box of "Not Invented Here": Attitudes, decision biases, and behavioral consequences. *Academy of Management Perspectives, 29*(2), 193–217.

Argyres, N., & McGahan, A. M. (2002). An interview with Michael Porter. *Academy of Management Perspectives, 16*(2), 43–52.

Argyris, C. (1976). Single-loop and double-loop models in research on decision making. *Administrative Science Quarterly, 21*(3), 363–375.

Armenakis, A. A., Harris, S. G., & Mossholder, K. W. (1993). Creating readiness for organizational change. *Human Relations, 46*(6), 681–703.

Armour, H. O., & Teece, D. J. (1978). Organizational structure and economic performance: A test of the multidivisional hypothesis. *Bell Journal of Economics, 9*(1), 106–122.

References

Arrow, K. J. (1973). Information and economic behavior. Technical Report No. 14. Cambridge, MA: Harvard University. https://apps.dtic.mil/sti/tr/pdf/AD0768446.pdf (accessed December 20, 2023).

Arthur, W. B. (2023). Economics in nouns and verbs. *Journal of Economic Behavior & Organization, 205*, 638–647.

Augier, M., & Teece, D. J. (2009). Dynamic capabilities and the role of managers in business strategy and economic performance. *Organization Science, 20*(2), 410–421.

Bain, J. S. (1959). *Industrial Organization*. New York: Wiley.

Barnett, W. P. (2008). *The Red Queen Among Organizations: How Competitiveness Evolves*. Princeton: Princeton University Press.

Barnett, W. P., & Hansen, M. T. (1996). The red queen in organizational evolution. *Strategic Management Journal, 17*(S1), 139–157.

Baron, R. A., & Ensley, M. D. (2006). Opportunity recognition as the detection of meaningful patterns: Evidence from comparisons of novice and experienced entrepreneurs. *Management Science, 52*(9), 1331–1344.

Bass, B. M. (1985). *Leadership and Performance Beyond Expectations*. New York: Free Press.

Becker, F. (2007). Organizational ecology and knowledge networks. *California Management Review, 49*(2), 42–61.

Beer, M., & Nohria, N. (2000). Cracking the code of change. *Harvard Business Review, 78*(3), 133–141.

Benner, M. J., & Tushman, M. L. (2003). Exploitation, exploration, and process management: The productivity dilemma revisited. *Academy of Management Review, 28*(2), 238–256.

Bercovitz, J. E., de Figueiredo, J. M., & Teece, D. J. (1997). Firm capabilities and managerial decision making: A theory of innovation biases. In R. Garud, P. Nayyar, & Z. Shapira (eds.), *Technological Innovation: Oversights and Foresights*. Cambridge: Cambridge University Press, 233–259.

Berger, E. (2024). Some European launch officials still have their heads stuck in the sand. *ArsTechnica*, June 26, 2024. https://arstechnica.com/space/2024/06/some-european-launch-officials-still-have-their-heads-stuck-in-the-sand/.

Bhuiyan, N., & Baghel, A. (2005). An overview of continuous improvement: From the past to the present. *Management Decision, 43*(5), 761–771.

Bingham, C. B., & Eisenhardt, K. M. (2011). Rational heuristics: The "simple rules" that strategists learn from process experience. *Strategic Management Journal, 32*(13), 1437–1464.

Birkinshaw, J., & Ansari, S. (2015). Understanding management models: Going beyond "what" and "why" to "how" work gets done in organizations. In

N. J. Foss & T. Saebi (eds.), *Business Model Innovation: The Organizational Dimension*. Oxford: Oxford University Press, 85–103.

Blank, S. (2013). Why the lean start-up changes everything. *Harvard Business Review, 91*(5), 63–72.

Blank, S., & Dorf, B. (2020). *The Startup Owner's Manual: The Step-By-Step Guide for Building a Great Company*. Hoboken, NJ: John Wiley & Sons.

Bloom, N., Genakos, C., Sadun, R., & Van Reenen, J. (2012). Management practices across firms and countries. *Academy of Management Perspectives, 26*(1), 12–33.

Boulding, K. E. (1984). The fallacy of trends: On living with unpredictability. *National Forum, 64*(3), 19.

Brown, T. (2008). Design thinking. *Harvard Business Review, 86*(6), 84–92.

Brown, T. (2009). *Change by Design: How Design Thinking Transforms Organizations and Inspires Innovation*. New York: HarperBusiness.

Brown, T., & Martin, R. (2014). Capitalism needs design thinking. IDEO. www.ideo.com/post/capitalism-needs-design-thinking (accessed September 19, 2022).

Burke, A., Van Stel, A., & Thurik, R. (2016). Testing the validity of blue ocean strategy versus competitive strategy: An analysis of the retail industry. *International Review of Entrepreneurship, 14*(2), 123–146.

Casson, M., & Godley, A. (2007). Revisiting the emergence of the modern business enterprise: entrepreneurship and the Singer global distribution system. *Journal of Management Studies, 44*(7), 1064–1077.

Caves, R. E., & Porter, M. E. (1977). From entry barriers to mobility barriers: Conjectural decisions and contrived deterrence to new competition. *Quarterly Journal of Economics, 91*(2), 241–261.

Chambers, J. (2017). Turning setbacks into success. *linkedin.com*, April 17, 2017. www.linkedin.com/pulse/turning-setbacks-success-john-chambers (accessed December 30, 2019).

Chandler, A. D. (1977). *The Visible Hand*. Cambridge, MA: Harvard University Press.

Chen, J. (2023). CEO tenure rates. *Harvard Law School Forum on Corporate Governance*. https://corpgov.law.harvard.edu/2023/08/04/ceo-tenure-rates-2/.

Chesbrough, H. W. (2003). *Open Innovation: The New Imperative for Creating and Profiting from Technology*. Boston, MA: Harvard Business School Press.

Chesbrough, H., & Tucci, C. L. (2020). The interplay between open innovation and lean startup, or, why large companies are not large versions of startups. *Strategic Management Review, 1*(2), 277–303.

Chopoorian, R., & Gross, D. (2021). Pfizer's vaccine machine. *strategy + business, 2021*(102). www.strategy-business.com/article/Pfizers-vaccine-machine.

Christensen, C. (1997). *The Innovator's Dilemma*. Boston, MA: Harvard Business School Press.

Christensen, C. M., & Bower, J. L. (1996). Customer power, strategic investment, and the failure of leading firms. *Strategic Management Journal, 17*(3), 197–218.

Christensen, C. M., & Raynor, M. E. (2003). *The Innovator's Solution: Creating and Sustaining Successful Growth*. Boston, MA: Harvard Business School Press.

Churchman, C. W. (1968) *The Systems Approach*. New York: Dell.

Citrin, J. M., Hildebrand, C. A., & Stark, R. J. (2019). The CEO life cycle. *Harvard Business Review, 97*(6), 56–60.

Clark, K. B., & Fujimoto, T. (1990). *Product Development Performance: Strategy, Organization, and Management in the World Auto Industry*. Boston, MA: Harvard Business School Press.

Cornelius, P., Van de Putte, A., & Romani, M. (2005). Three decades of scenario planning in Shell. *California Management Review, 48*(1), 92–109.

Cross, N., Dorst, K., & Roozenburg, N. (eds.) (1992) *Research in Design Thinking*. Delft, Netherlands: Delft University Press.

d-school (2010). An Introduction to Design Thinking: Process Guide. Hasso Plattner Institute of Design at Stanford. https://web.stanford.edu/~mshanks/MichaelShanks/files/509554.pdf (accessed October 20, 2024).

Danneels, E., & Vestal, A. (2020). Normalizing vs. analyzing: Drawing the lessons from failure to enhance firm innovativeness. *Journal of Business Venturing, 35*(1), 105903. https://doi.org/10.1016/j.jbusvent.2018.10.001.

Davis, I., & Dickson, T. (2014). Lou Gerstner on corporate reinvention and values. *McKinsey Quarterly*, 2014(3), 123–129. www.mckinsey.com/featured-insights/leadership/lou-gerstner-on-corporate-reinvention-and-values.

Day, G. S., & Schoemaker, P. J. H. (2006). *Peripheral Vision: Detecting the Weak Signals that Will Make or Break Your Company*. Cambridge, MA: Harvard Business School Press.

De Figueiredo, J. M., & Teece, D. J. (1996). Mitigating procurement hazards in the context of innovation. *Industrial and Corporate Change, 5*(2), 537–559.

Demsetz, H. (1973). Industry structure, market rivalry, and public policy. *Journal of Law & Economics, 16*(1), 1–9.

Deutschman, A. (2004). Inside the mind of Jeff Bezos. *Fast Company*, August, (85), 52–58.

Di Stefano, G., Peteraf, M., & Verona, G. (2010). Dynamic capabilities deconstructed: a bibliographic investigation into the origins, development, and future directions of the research domain. *Industrial and Corporate Change, 19*(4), 1187–1204.

Dooley, R. S. & Fryxell, G. E. (1999). Attaining decision quality and commitment from dissent: The moderating effects of loyalty and competence in strategic decision-making teams. *Academy of Management Journal*, *42*(4), 389–402.

Dorst, K. (2011). The core of "design thinking" and its application. *Design Studies*, *32*(6), 521–532.

Eisenhardt, K. M., & Martin, J. A. (2000). Dynamic capabilities: What are they? *Strategic Management Journal*, *21*(10–11), 1105–1121.

Felin, T., Gambardella, A., Stern, S., & Zenger, T. (2020). Lean startup and the business model: Experimentation revisited. *Long Range Planning*, *53*(4), 101889. https://doi.org/10.1016/j.lrp.2019.06.002.

Fisk, P. (2017). Design thinking in action . . . 35 great examples of companies using "design thinking" to drive innovation and growth. www.peterfisk.com/2017/05/design-thinking-in-action-35-great-examples-of-companies-using-design-thinking-to-drive-innovation-and-growth/ (accessed September 21, 2022).

Frier, S. (2020). Documents show Facebook bought Instagram to quash competitor, *Bloomberg*, July 29, 2020. www.bloomberg.com/news/articles/2020-07-29/documents-show-facebook-bought-instagram-to-quash-competitor (accessed October 23, 2023).

Gavetti, G. (2005). Cognition and hierarchy: Rethinking the microfoundations of capabilities' development. *Organization Science*, *16*(6), 599–617.

Gavetti, G. (2012). Perspective: Toward a behavioral theory of strategy. *Organization Science*, *23*(1), 267–285.

Gernone, F. & Teece, D. J. (2024). Competing in the age of AI: Firm capabilities and antitrust considerations. In A. Abbott & T. Schrepel (eds.), *Artificial Intelligence and Competition Policy*. Paris: Concurrences, 17–34.

Gibbons, R., & Henderson, R. (2012). Relational contracts and organizational capabilities. *Organization Science*, *23*(5), 1350–1364.

Gratton, L., & Ghoshal, S. (2005). Beyond best practice. *MIT Sloan Management Review*, *46*(3), 49–57.

Grewal, R., & Slotegraaf, R. J. (2007). Embeddedness of organizational capabilities. *Decision Sciences*, *38*(3), 451–488.

Grove, A. S. (1996). *Only the Paranoid Survive: How to Exploit the Crisis Points That Challenge Every Company and Career*. New York: Currency Doubleday.

Hamel, G. (1991). Competition for competence and interpartner learning within international strategic alliances. *Strategic Management Journal*, *12*(S1), 83–103.

Hamel, G., & Prahalad, C. K. (1993). Strategy as stretch and leverage. *Harvard Business Review*, *71*(2), 75–84.

Hanson, N. R. (1958). *Patterns of Discovery: An Inquiry into the Conceptual Foundations of Science*. Cambridge: Cambridge University Press.

Harvey, J.-F. (2022). Microfoundations of sensing capabilities: From managerial cognition to team behavior. *Strategic Organization* (Online First). https://doi.org/10.1177/14761270221142959.

He, Z. L., & Wong, P. K. (2004). Exploration vs. exploitation: An empirical test of the ambidexterity hypothesis. *Organization Science*, *15*(4), 481–494.

Helfat, C. E., & Martin, J. A. (2015). Dynamic managerial capabilities: Review and assessment of managerial impact on strategic change. *Journal of Management*, *41*(5), 1281–1312.

Helfat, C. E., & Peteraf, M. A. (2003). The dynamic resource-based view: Capability lifecycles. *Strategic Management Journal*, *24*(10), 997–1010.

Helfat, C. E., & Peteraf, M. A. (2009). Understanding dynamic capabilities: Progress along a developmental path. *Strategic Organization*, *7*(1): 91–102.

Helfat, C. E., & Peteraf, M. A. (2015). Managerial cognitive capabilities and the microfoundations of dynamic capabilities. *Strategic Management Journal*, *36*(6), 831–850.

Helfat, C. E., & Raubitschek, R. S. (2000). Product sequencing: Co-evolution of knowledge, capabilities and products. *Strategic Management Journal*, *21*(10–11), 961–979.

Helfat, C. E., & Winter, S. G. (2011). Untangling dynamic and operational capabilities: Strategy for the (N)ever-changing world. *Strategic Management Journal*, *32*(11), 1243–1250.

Henderson, R. M. (1994). Managing innovation in the information age. *Harvard Business Review*, 72(1), 100–106.

Henderson, R. (2006). The innovator's dilemma as a problem of organizational competence. *Journal of Product Innovation Management*, *23*(1), 5–11.

Henderson, R. M., & Clark, K. B. (1990). Architectural innovation: The reconfiguration of existing product technologies and the failure of established firms. *Administrative Science Quarterly*, *35*(1), 9–30.

High, P. (2018). Former Cisco CEO John Chambers is trying to change the world. *Forbes.com*, December 3, 2018. www.forbes.com/sites/peterhigh/2018/12/03/former-cisco-ceo-john-chambers-is-trying-to-change-the-world/#7696dcbd4364 (accessed December 29, 2019).

Hill, T., & Westbrook, R. (1997). SWOT analysis: It's time for a product recall. *Long Range Planning*, *30*(1), 46–52.

Hodgkinson, G. P., & Healey, M. P. (2011). Psychological foundations of dynamic capabilities: Reflexion and reflection in strategic management. *Strategic Management Journal*, *32*(13), 1500–1516.

Hsieh, T. (2017). Safe enough to try: An interview with Zappos CEO Tony Hsieh. *McKinsey.com*, October 19. www.mckinsey.com/capabilities/people-and-organizational-performance/our-insights/safe-enough-to-try-an-interview-with-zappos-ceo-tony-hsieh (accessed June 23, 2023).

Humphrey, A. S. (2005). SWOT Analysis for management consulting. *SRI International Alumni Association Newsletter*, December. https://alumni.sri.com/newsletters/2005/AlumNews-Dec-2005.pdf (accessed October 20, 2022).

Ignatius, A. (2015). How Indra Nooyi turned design thinking into strategy: An interview with PepsiCo's CEO. *Harvard Business Review, 93*(9), 80–85.

Ignatius, A. (2017). We need people to lean into the future. *Harvard Business Review, 95*(2), 94–100.

Ireland, R. D., Covin, J. G., & Kuratko, D. F. 2009. Conceptualizing corporate entrepreneurship strategy. *Entrepreneurship Theory and Practice, 33*(1), 19–46.

Jackson, S. E., & Dutton, J. E. (1988). Discerning threats and opportunities. *Administrative Science Quarterly, 33*(3), 370–387.

Jansen, J. J., George, G., Van den Bosch, F. A., & Volberda, H. W. (2008). Senior team attributes and organizational ambidexterity: The moderating role of transformational leadership. *Journal of Management Studies, 45*(5), 982–1007.

Jargon, J. (2017) How Panera solved its "mosh pit" problem. *Wall Street Journal*, June 2. www.wsj.com/articles/how-panera-solved-its-mosh-pit-problem-1496395801 (accessed December 20, 2023).

Johnson, S. (1998). *Who Moved My Cheese? An Amazing Way to Deal with Change in Your Work and in Your Life*. New York: Putnam.

Kahneman, D., Lovallo, D., & Sibony, O. (2011). Before you make that big decision. *Harvard Business Review, 89*(6), 50–60.

Kaplan, S., & Beinhocker, E. D. (2003). The real value of strategic planning. *MIT Sloan Management Review, 44*(2), 71–76.

Karim, S. (2006). Modularity in organizational structure: The reconfiguration of internally developed and acquired business units. *Strategic Management Journal, 27*(9), 799–823.

Karim, S., & Mitchell, W. (2000). Path-dependent and path-breaking change: reconfiguring business resources following acquisitions in the US medical sector, 1978–1995. *Strategic Management Journal, 21*(10–11), 1061–1081.

Katzenbach, J. R., Steffen, I., & Kronley, C. (2012). Cultural change that sticks. *Harvard Business Review, 90*(7), 110–117.

Kelley, T. & Kelley, D. (2013). *Creative Confidence: Unlocking the Creative Potential Within Us All*. New York: Crown Business.

Kim, W. C., & Mauborgne, R. (2005). *Blue Ocean Strategy: How to Create Uncontested Market Space and Make the Competition Irrelevant*. Boston, MA: Harvard Business School Press.

Kirzner, I. M. (1973). *Competition and Entrepreneurship*. Chicago: University of Chicago Press.

Kirzner, I. M. (1985). Uncertainty, discovery, and human action. In I. M. Kirzner (ed.), *Discovery and the Capitalist Process*. Chicago, IL: Chicago University Press, 40–67.

Klayman, J., Soll, J. B., Gonzalez-Vallejo, C., & Barlas, S. (1999). Overconfidence: It depends on how, what, and whom you ask. *Organizational Behavior and Human Decision Processes*, *79*(3), 216–247.

Knowledge at Wharton (2018). The downside of applying lean startup principles. https://knowledge.wharton.upenn.edu/article/the-limitations-of-lean-startup-principles/ (accessed June 23, 2022).

Kolko, J. (2015). Design thinking comes of age. *Harvard Business Review*, *93*(9), 66–71.

Kotter, J. P. (1995). Leading change: Why transformation efforts fail. *Harvard Business Review*, *73*(2), 59–67.

Kupp, M., Anderson, J., & Reckhenrich, J. (2017). Why design thinking in business needs a rethink. *MIT Sloan Management Review*, *59*(1), 42–44.

Lancefield, D., & Gross, D. (2020). The clear Sky strategy. *strategy + business*, issue 100. www.strategy-business.com/article/The-clear-Sky-strategy (accessed December 20, 2023)

Lee, M. Y., & Edmondson, A. C. (2017). Self-managing organizations: Exploring the limits of less-hierarchical organizing. *Research in Organizational Behavior*, *37*, 35–58.

Leih, S., & Teece, D. (2016). Campus leadership and the entrepreneurial university: A dynamic capabilities perspective. *Academy of Management Perspectives*, *30*(2), 182–210.

Levitt, B., & March, J. G. (1988). Organizational learning. *Annual Review of Sociology*, *14*(1), 319–338.

Lichtenthaler, U., & Lichtenthaler, E. (2009). A capability-based framework for open innovation: Complementing absorptive capacity. *Journal of Management Studies*, *46*(8), 1315–1338.

Liedtka, J. (2018). Why design thinking works. *Harvard Business Review*, *96*(5), 72–79.

Lippman, S. A., & Rumelt, R. P. (1982). Uncertain imitability: An analysis of interfirm differences in efficiency under competition. *Bell Journal of Economics*, 418–438.

Lohr, S., & Clark, D. (2024). How Intel got left behind in the A.I. chip boom. *New York Times*, October 24. www.nytimes.com/2024/10/24/technology/intel-ai-chips-mistakes.html.

Lorange, P. (1980). *Corporate Planning: An Executive Viewpoint*. Englewood Cliffs, NJ: Prentice-Hall.

Lovallo, D., Brown, A. L., Teece, D. J., & Bardolet, D. (2020). Resource reallocation capabilities in internal capital markets: The value of overcoming inertia. *Strategic Management Journal*, *41*(8), 1365–1380.

Lutz, B. (2011). Life lessons from the car guy. WSJ.com, June 11, 2011. www.wsj.com/articles/SB10001424052702304259304576375790237203556 (accessed December 29, 2019).

Malone, T. W. (2004). *The Future of Work: How the New Order of Business Will Shape Your Organization, Your Management Style, and Your Life*. Boston, MA: Harvard Business School Press.

March, J. G. (1991). Exploration and exploitation in organizational learning. *Organization Science*, *2*(1), 71–87.

Markides, C. (2006). Disruptive innovation: In need of better theory. *Journal of Product Innovation Management*, *23*(1), 19–25.

Martin, R. (2009). *The Design of Business: Why Design Thinking Is the Next Competitive Advantage*. Cambridge, MA: Harvard Business Press.

Mason, E. S. (1949). The current state of the monopoly problem in the United States. *Harvard Law Review*, *62*(8), 1265–1285.

Mazzucato, M., & Kattel, R. (2020). COVID-19 and public-sector capacity. *Oxford Review of Economic Policy*, *36*(Supplement_4), S256–S269.

Mazzucato, M., Qobo, M., & Kattel, R. (2022). Building state capacities and dynamic capabilities to drive social and economic development: The case of South Africa. In M. Qobo, M. Soko, & N. X. Ngwenya (eds.), *The Future of the South African Political Economy Post-COVID 19*. Cham, Switzerland: Palgrave Macmillan, 43–74.

McGrath, R. (2020). The new disrupters. *MIT Sloan Management Review*, *61*(3), 28–33.

McGrath, R. G. (2013). *The End of Competitive Advantage: How to Keep Your Strategy Moving as Fast as Your Business*. Boston, MA: Harvard Business School Press.

McTaggart, J. M., Kontes, P.W., & Mankins, M. C. (1994). *The Value Imperative: Managing for Superior Shareholder Returns*. New York: Free Press.

Mintzberg, H. (1994). The fall and rise of strategic planning. *Harvard Business Review*, *72*(1), 107–114.

Mintzberg, H., & McHugh, A. (1985). Strategy formation in an adhocracy. *Administrative Science Quarterly, 30*(2), 160–197.

Mintzberg, H., Raisinghani, D., & Theoret, A. (1976). The structure of "unstructured" decision processes. *Administrative Science Quarterly, 21*(2), 246–275.

Murmann, J., & Vogt, F. (2023). A capabilities framework for dynamic competition: Assessing the relative chances of incumbents, start-ups, and diversifying entrants. *Management and Organization Review, 19*(1), 141–156.

Nadler, D. A., & Tushman, M. L. (1977). A general diagnostic model for organization behavior, in J. R. Hackman, E. E. Lawler, & L. W. Porter (eds.), *Perspectives on Behavior in Organizations*. New York: McGraw-Hill, 112–126.

Nadler, D. A., & Tushman, M. L. (1980). A model for diagnosing organizational behavior. *Organizational Dynamics, 9*(2), 35–51.

Nadler, D. A. & Tushman, M. L. (1989). Organizational frame bending: Principles for managing reorientation. *Academy of Management Executive, 3*(3), 194–204.

Nadler, D. A., & Tushman, M. L. (1997). *Competing by Design: The Power of Organizational Architecture*. New York: Oxford University Press.

Nijstad, B. A., Berger-Selman, F., & De Dreu, C. K. (2014). Innovation in top management teams: Minority dissent, transformational leadership, and radical innovations. *European Journal of Work and Organizational Psychology, 23*(2), 310–322.

Nonaka, I. (1991). The knowledge-creating company. *Harvard Business Review, 69*(6), 96–104.

Nonaka, I. (1994). A dynamic theory of organizational knowledge creation, *Organization Science, 5*(1), 14–37.

Nonaka, I., & Takeuchi, H. (1995), *The Knowledge-creating Company*. Oxford: Oxford University Press.

Nonaka, I., & Takeuchi, H. (2011). The wise leader. *Harvard Business Review, 89*(5), 58–67.

Nonaka, I., Toyama, R., & Konno, N. (2000). SECI, Ba and leadership: a unified model of dynamic knowledge creation. *Long Range Planning, 33*(1), 5–34.

Ogilvy, J., & Schwartz, P. (2004). *Plotting Your Scenarios*. Emeryville, CA: Global Business Network. http://adaptknowledge.com/wp-content/uploads/rapidintake/PI_CL/media/gbn_Plotting_Scenarios.pdf (accessed March 6, 2019).

O'Reilly, C. A. & Tushman, M. L. (2004). The ambidextrous organization. *Harvard Business Review*, 82(4), 74–81.

O'Reilly, C. A. & Tushman, M. L. (2008). Ambidexterity as a dynamic capability: Resolving the innovator's dilemma, in A. P. Brief & B. M. Staw (eds.), *Research in Organizational Behavior*, vol. 28. Oxford: Elsevier, 185–206.

Osterwalder, A., & Pigneur, Y. (2010). *Business Model Generation: A Handbook for Visionaries, Game Changers, and Challengers*. Hoboken, NJ: Wiley.

Ostrom, E. (2010). Beyond markets and states: Polycentric governance of complex economic systems. In K. Grandin (ed.), *The Nobel Prizes 2009*. Stockholm: Norstedts Tryckeri, 408–444. www.nobelprize.org/uploads/2018/06/ostrom_lecture.pdf (accessed March 12, 2023).

Overholt, M. H. (1997). Flexible organizations: Using organizational design as a competitive advantage. *People and Strategy*, 20(1), 22–32.

Penenberg, A. L. (2012). Reid Hoffman on PayPal's pivoted path to success. *Fast Company*, August 9, 2012. www.fastcompany.com/1837839/reid-hoffman-paypals-pivoted-path-success (accessed March 12, 2023).

Peters, T. J. & Waterman. Jr., R. H. (1982). *In Search of Excellence: Lessons from America's Best-Run Companies*. New York: Harper & Row.

Phillips, A. (1971). *Technology and Market Structure: A Study of the Aircraft Industry*. Lexington, MA: Heath Lexington Books.

Pisano, G. P., & Teece, D. J. (2007). How to capture value from innovation: Shaping intellectual property and industry architecture. *California Management Review*, 50(1), 278–296.

Porter, M. (1980). *Competitive Strategy*. New York: Free Press.

Porter, M. (1991). How competitive forces shape strategy. In C. Montgomery & M. Porter (eds.), *Strategy: Seeking and Securing Competitive Advantage*. Boston, MA: Harvard Business School Press, 11–26.

Powell, T. C. (1995). Total quality management as competitive advantage: A review and empirical study. *Strategic Management Journal*, 16(1), 15–37.

Redding, J. (1997). Hardwiring the learning organization. *Training & Development*, 51(8), 61–68.

Reeves, M., Love, C., & Tillmanns, P. (2012). Your strategy needs a strategy. *Harvard Business Review*, 90(9), 76–83.

Ries, E. (2011). *The Lean Startup: How Today's Entrepreneurs Use Continuous Innovation to Create Radically Successful Businesses*. New York: Crown Business.

Ries, E. (2017). *The Startup Way: How Modern Companies Use Entrepreneurial Management to Transform Culture and Drive Long-Term Growth*. New York: Currency.

Ringland, G. (1998). *Scenario Planning: Managing for the Future*. Chichester: John Wiley & Sons.

Ritter, T. (2014). *Alignment² [Alignment-squared]: Driving Competitiveness and Growth through Business Model Excellence*. Frederiksberg, Denmark: CBS Competitiveness Platform.

Romanelli, E., & Tushman, M. L. (1994). Organizational transformation as punctuated equilibrium: An empirical test. *Academy of Management Journal*, *37*(5), 1141–1166.

Rose, G. (2013). Generation kill: A conversation with Stanley McChrystal. *Foreign Affairs*, *92*(4), 2–8.

Rowe, P. G. (1987). *Design Thinking*. Cambridge, MA: The MIT Press.

Rule, J. N. (2013). A symbiotic relationship: The OODA loop, intuition, and strategic thought. Carlisle Barracks, PA: U.S. Army War College. https://apps.dtic.mil/dtic/tr/fulltext/u2/a590672.pdf (accessed March 12, 2023).

Rumelt, R. (1984). Towards a strategic theory of the firm. In R. B. Lamb (ed.), *Competitive Strategic Management*. Englewood Cliffs, NJ: Prentice-Hall, 556–570.

Rumelt, R. P. (1991). How much does industry matter? *Strategic Management Journal*, *12*(3), 167–185.

Rumelt, R. (2011), *Good Strategy/Bad Strategy: The Difference and Why It Matters*. New York: Crown Business.

Rumelt, R. P., Schendel, D., & Teece, D. J. (1991). Strategic management and economics. *Strategic Management Journal*, *12*(S2), 5–29.

Samson, D., & Terziovski, M. (1999). The relationship between total quality management practices and operational performance. *Journal of Operations Management*, *17*(4), 393–409.

Samuelson, W., & Zeckhauser, R. (1988). Status quo bias in decision making. *Journal of Risk and Uncertainty*, *1*(1), 7–59.

Schendel, D. E., & Hatten, K. J. (1972). Business policy or strategic management: A broader view for an emerging discipline. Institute for Research in the Behavioral, Economic, and Management Sciences, Paper No. 371. Purdue University. https://files.eric.ed.gov/fulltext/ED102732.pdf (accessed March 12, 2023).

Schilke, O., Hu, Songcui, & Helfat, C. E. (2018). Quo vadis, dynamic capabilities? A content-analytic review of the current state of knowledge and recommendations for future research. *Academy of Management Annals*, *12*(1), 390–439.

Schoemaker, P. J. (1992). How to link strategic vision to core capabilities. *Sloan Management Review*, *34*, 67–81.

Schoemaker, P. J. (1993). Multiple scenario development: Its conceptual and behavioral foundation. *Strategic Management Journal*, *14*(3), 193–213.

Schoemaker, P. J. (2004). Forecasting and scenario planning: The challenges of uncertainty and complexity. In D. J. Koehler & N. Harvey (eds.), *Blackwell*

Handbook of Judgment and Decision Making. Malden, MA: Blackwell, 274–296.

Schoemaker, P. J. (2022). *Advanced Introduction to Scenario Planning*. Cheltenham: Edward Elgar.

Schoemaker, P. J., Heaton, S., & Teece, D. (2018). Innovation, dynamic capabilities, and leadership. *California Management Review, 61*(1), 15–42.

Schön, O. (2012). Business model modularity – a way to gain strategic flexibility? *Controlling & Management, 56*(2), 73–78.

Scoblic, J. P. (2020). Learning from the future. *Harvard Business Review, 98*(4), 38–47.

Sellers, P., & Kirkpatrick, D. (1993). Can this man save IBM? *Fortune, 127*(8), April 19, 63–67.

Senge, P. M. (1990). The leader's new work: Building leading organization. *Sloan Management Review, 32*(1), 7–23.

Senge, P. M. (2006). *The Fifth Discipline: The Art and Practice of the Learning Organization, Revised 2nd Edition*. New York: Doubleday/Currency.

Servan-Schreiber, J.-J. (1968). *The American Challenge*. New York: Atheneum.

Simon, H. A. (1969). *The Sciences of the Artificial*. Cambridge, MA: MIT Press.

Smith, A. (1776). *An Inquiry into the Nature and Causes of the Wealth of Nations*. London: Methuen.

Stone, M. (2015). A 2004 email from Jeff Bezos explains why PowerPoint presentations aren't allowed at Amazon. *Business Insider*, July 28, 2015. www.businessinsider.com/jeff-bezos-email-against-powerpoint-presentations-2015-7 (accessed February 22, 2022).

Stopford, J. M., & Baden-Fuller, C. W. (1994). Creating corporate entrepreneurship. *Strategic Management Journal, 15*(7), 521–536.

Sugimori, Y., Kusunoki, K., Cho, F., & Uchikawa, S. (1977). Toyota production system and kanban system materialization of just-in-time and respect-for-human system. *International Journal of Production Research, 15*(6), 553–564.

Sutton, J. (2012). *Competing in Capabilities: The Globalization Process*. Oxford: Oxford University Press.

Syverson, C. (2011). What determines productivity? *Journal of Economic Literature, 49*, 326–365.

Tedlow, R. S. (1988). The struggle for dominance in the automobile market: The early years of Ford and General Motors. *Business and Economic History, 17*, 49–62.

Teece, D. J. (1984). Economic analysis and strategic management. *California Management Review, 26*(3), 87–110.

Teece, D. J. (1986). Profiting from technological innovation: Implications for integration, collaboration, licensing and public policy. *Research Policy*, *15*(6), 285–305.

Teece, D. J. (2006). Reflections on "profiting from innovation". *Research Policy*, *35*(8), 1131–1146.

Teece, D. J. (2007). Explicating dynamic capabilities: The nature and microfoundations of (sustainable) enterprise performance. *Strategic Management Journal*, *28*(13), 1319–1350.

Teece, D. J. (2010a). Business models, business strategy and innovation. *Long Range Planning*, *43*(2–3), 172–194.

Teece, D. J. (2010b). Technological innovation and the theory of the firm: The role of enterprise-level knowledge, complementarities, and (dynamic) capabilities. In N. Rosenberg & B. H. Hall (eds.), *Handbook of the Economics of Innovation, Vol.1*. Oxford: North-Holland, 679–730.

Teece, D. J. (2014). The foundations of enterprise performance: Dynamic and ordinary capabilities in an (economic) theory of firms. *Academy of Management Perspectives*, *28*(4), 328–352.

Teece, D. J. (2015). Intangible assets and a theory of heterogeneous firms. In A. Bounfour & T. Miyagawa (eds.), *Intangibles, Market Failure and Innovation Performance*. New York: Springer, 217–239.

Teece, D. J. (2016a). Dynamic capabilities and entrepreneurial management in large organizations: Toward a theory of the (entrepreneurial) firm. *European Economic Review*, *86*, 202–216.

Teece, D. J. (2016b). Co-specialization. In M. Augier & D. J. Teece (eds.), *The Palgrave Encyclopedia of Strategic Management*. London: Palgrave Macmillan. https://doi.org/10.1057/978-1-349-94848-2_471-1.

Teece, D. J. (2017). Dynamic capabilities and (digital) platform lifecycles. In J. Furman, A. Gawer, B. Silverman, & S. Stern (eds.), *Entrepreneurship, Innovation, and Platforms*. Bingley: Emerald, 211–225.

Teece, D. J. (2018a). Dynamic capabilities as (workable) management systems theory. *Journal of Management & Organization*, *24*(3), 359–368.

Teece, D. J. (2018b). Business models and dynamic capabilities. *Long Range Planning*, *51*(1), 40–49.

Teece, D. J. (2018c). Capability development. In M. Augier & D. J. Teece (eds.), *The Palgrave Encyclopedia of Strategic Management*. London: Palgrave Macmillan, 192–194. https://doi.org/10.1057/978-1-137-00772-8_572.

Teece, D. J. (2019a). Strategic renewal and dynamic capabilities: Managing uncertainty, irreversibilities, and congruence. In A. Tuncdogan, A. Lindgreen, F. Van Den Bosch, & H. Volberda (eds.), *Strategic Renewal: Core Concepts, Antecedents, and Micro Foundations*. London: Routledge, 21–51.

Teece, D. J. (2019b). A capability theory of the firm: An economics and (strategic) management perspective. *New Zealand Economic Papers*, *53*(1), 1–43.

Teece, D. J. (2019c). China and the reshaping of the auto industry: A dynamic capabilities perspective. *Management and Organization Review*, *15*(1), 177–199.

Teece, D. J. (2020). Hand in glove: Open innovation and the dynamic capabilities framework. *Strategic Management Review*, *1*(2), 233–253.

Teece, D. J. (2022a). A wider-aperture lens for global strategic management: The multinational enterprise in a bifurcated global economy. *Global Strategy Journal*, *12*(3), 488–519.

Teece, D. J. (2022b). The evolution of the dynamic capabilities framework. In R. Adams, D. Grichnik, A. Pundziene, & C. Volkmann (eds.), *Artificiality and Sustainability in Entrepreneurship*. Cham, Switzerland: Springer, 113–129.

Teece, D. J. (2023). The dynamic competition paradigm: Insights and implications. *Columbia Business Law Review*, *2023*(1), 373–461.

Teece, D. J. (2025). Understanding dynamic competition: New perspectives on potential competition, "monopoly," and market power. *Antitrust Law Journal*, *86*(3), 735–803.

Teece, D. J., Gupta, K., & Rosenberg, D. J. (2023). New priorities of corporate Directors: Geopolitical and Technological Disruptions. *International In-house Counsel Journal*, *16*(63), 8401–8408.

Teece, D., Peteraf, M., & Leih, S. (2016). Dynamic capabilities and organizational agility: Risk, uncertainty, and strategy in the innovation economy. *California Management Review*, *58*(4), 13–35.

Teece, D., & Pisano, G. (1994). The dynamic capabilities of firms: An introduction. *Industrial and Corporate Change*, *3*(3), 537–556.

Teece, D. J., Pisano, G., & Shuen, A. (1990). Firm capabilities, resources, and the concept of strategy. CCC Working Paper 90–8, Center for Research in Management. University of California.

Teece, D. J., Pisano, G., & Shuen, A. (1997). Dynamic capabilities and strategic management. *Strategic Management Journal*, *18*(7), 509–533.

Teece, D. J., Pundziene, A., Heaton, S., & Vadi, M. (2022). Managing Multi-Sided Platforms: Platform Origins and Go-to-Market Strategy. *California Management Review*, *64*(4), 5–19.

Teece, D. J., Raspin, P. G., & Cox, D. R. (2020). Plotting strategy in a dynamic world. *MIT Sloan Management Review*, *62*(1), 28–33.

Tetlock, P. E., & Gardner, D. (2015). *Superforecasting: The Art and Science of Prediction*. New York: Crown.

Thomas, O. (2018). Two decades of cognitive bias research in entrepreneurship: What do we know and where do we go from here? *Management Review Quarterly*, *68*(2), 107–143.

Tilley, A. (2024). How Apple fell behind in the AI arms race. *Wall Street Journal*, June 5. www.wsj.com/tech/ai/apple-ai-siri-development-behind-9ea65ee8.

Tushman, M. L., & O'Reilly, C. A. (1996). The ambidextrous organization: Managing evolutionary and revolutionary change. *California Management Review*, *38*, 1–23.

Valentin, E. K. (2001). SWOT analysis from a resource-based view. *Journal of Marketing Theory and Practice*, *9*(2), 54–69.

Waterman Jr, R. H., Peters, T. J., & Phillips, J. R. (1980). Structure is not organization. *Business Horizons*, *23*(3), 14–26.

Watts, B., & Augier, M. (2022). John Boyd on competition and conflict. *Comparative Strategy*, *41*(3), 233–260.

Wernerfelt, B. (1984). A resource-based view of the firm. *Strategic Management Journal*, *5*(2), 171–180.

Williamson, O. E. (1975). *Markets and Hierarchies*. New York: Free Press.

Winter, S. G. (2000). The satisficing principle in capability learning. *Strategic Management Journal*, *21*(10–11), 981–996.

Winter, S. G. (2003). Understanding dynamic capabilities. *Strategic Management Journal*, *24*(10), 991–995.

Winter, S. G. (2017). Pursuing the evolutionary agenda in economics and management research. *Cambridge Journal of Economics*, *41*(3), 721–747.

Womack, J. P., Jones, D. T., & Roos, D. (1990). *The Machine That Changed the World: Based on the Massachusetts Institute of Technology 5-Million Dollar 5-Year Study on the Future of the Automobile*. New York: Rawson.

Zollo, M., & Winter, S. G. (2002). Deliberate learning and the evolution of dynamic capabilities. *Organization Science*, *13*(3), 339–351.

Zott, C., Amit, R., & Massa, L. (2011). The business model: Recent developments and future research. *Journal of Management*, *37*(4), 1019–1042.

Business Strategy

J.-C. Spender
Kozminski University
J.-C. Spender is a research Professor, Kozminski University. He has been active in the business strategy field since 1971 and is the author or co-author of 7 books and numerous papers. His principal academic interest is in knowledge-based theories of the private sector firm, and managing them.

Advisory Board

Jay Barney, *Eccles School of Business, The University of Utah*
Stewart Clegg, *University of Technology, Sydney*
Thomas Durand, *Conservatoire National des Arts et Métiers, Paris*
CT Foo, *Independent Scholar, Singapore*
Robert Grant, *Bocconi University, Milan*
Robin Holt, *Copenhagen Business School*
Paula Jarzabkowski, *Cass School, City University, London*
Naga Lakshmi Damaraju, *Indian School of Business*
Marjorie Lyles, *Kelley School of Business, Indiana University*
Joseph T. Mahoney, *College of Business, University of Illinois at Urbana-Champaign*
Nicolai Foss, *Bocconi University, Milan*
Andreas Scherer, *University of Zurich*
Deepak Somaya, *College of Business, University of Illinois at Urbana-Champaign*
Eduard van Gelderen, *Chief Investment Officer, APG, Amsterdam*

About the Series

Business strategy's reach is vast, and important too since wherever there is business activity there is strategizing. As a field, strategy has a long history from medieval and colonial times to today's developed and developing economies. This series offers a place for interesting and illuminating research including industry and corporate studies, strategizing in service industries, the arts, the public sector, and the new forms of Internet-based commerce. It also covers today's expanding gamut of analytic techniques.

Cambridge Elements

Business Strategy

Elements in the Series

Evolution of the Automobile Industry: A Capability-Architecture-Performance Approach
Takahiro Fujimoto

People Centric Innovation Ecosystem: Japanese Management and Practices
Yingying Zhang-Zhang and Takeo Kikkawa

Strategizing in the Polish Furniture Industry
Paulina Bednarz-Łuczewska

A Historical Review of Swedish Strategy Research and the Rigor-Relevance Gap
Thomas Kalling and Lars Bengtsson

Global Strategy in Our Age of Chaos: How Will the Multinational Firm Survive?
Stephen Tallman and Mitchell P. Koza

Strategizing With Institutional Theory
Harry Sminia

Effectuation: Rethinking Fundamental Concepts in the Social Sciences
Saras Sarasvathy

Behavioral Strategy: Exploring Microfoundations of Competitive Advantage
Nicolai J. Foss, Ambra Mazzelli and Libby Weber

Digital Assets: A Portfolio Perspective
Henrique Schneider

Diversification in the World of Data and AI
Gianvito Lanzolla and Constantinos Markides

Dynamic Capabilities Foundational Concepts
David J. Teece

Dynamic Capabilities and Related Paradigms
David J. Teece

A full series listing is available at: www.cambridge.org/EBUS

For EU product safety concerns, contact us at Calle de José Abascal, 56–1°, 28003 Madrid, Spain or eugpsr@cambridge.org.

www.ingramcontent.com/pod-product-compliance
Ingram Content Group UK Ltd.
Pitfield, Milton Keynes, MK11 3LW, UK
UKHW020443250925
463284UK00026B/1252